KEY FACTS

THE ENGLISH LEGAL SYSTEM

JACQUELINE MARTIN

Hodder & Stoughton

A MEMBER OF THE HODDER HEADLINE GROUP

Orders: please contact Bookpoint Ltd, 130 Milton Park, Abingdon, Oxon OX14 4SB.
Telephone: (44) 01235 827720, Fax: (44) 01235 400454. Lines are open from 9.00 – 6.00,
Monday to Saturday, with a 24-hour message answering service.
Email address: orders@bookpoint.co.uk

British Library Cataloguing in Publication Data
A catalogue record for this title is available from The British Library

ISBN 0 340 801794

First published 2001
Impression number   10 9 8 7 6 5 4 3 2
Year   2005 2004 2003 2002

Cover design by Stewart Larking
Typeset by Transet Limited, Coventry, England.
Printed in Great Britain for Hodder & Stoughton Educational, a division of Hodder Headline
Plc, 338 Euston Road, London NW1 3BH by Cox & Wyman Ltd, Reading, Berks.

CONTENTS

PREFACE

The Key Facts series is designed to give a clear view of each subject. This will be useful to students when tackling new topics and is invaluable as a revision aid. Most chapters open with an outline in diagram form of the points covered in that chapter. The points are then developed in list form to make learning easier. Supporting cases are given throughout by name, and for some complex areas the facts of cases are given to reinforce the point being made.

The topics covered for the English Legal System are suitable for students studying on a variety of courses, especially first year degree and foundation courses in law. The book also covers topics required for AS examinations.

The law is as I believe it to be on 1st August 2001.

CHAPTER 1

WHAT IS LAW?

1.1 THE NATURE OF LAW

1.1.1 Definition of law

A brief definition of law is difficult, but the following are some suggestions.

1. Law is a set of rules that plays an important part in the creation and maintenance of social order.
2. John Austin defined law as a command issued from a Sovereign power to an inferior and enforced by coercion.
3. Sir John Salmond defined law as being 'the body of principles recognised and applied by the State in the administration of justice'.
4. Law is a formal mechanism for controlling society, but it is not the only mechanism; less formal rules of morality and custom also play a part.

1.1.2 Law and morality

1. Morality is what is right and wrong according to a set of values or beliefs governing a group's behaviour.
2. Morality is not fixed and will vary from one group/society to another. Moral values may also change over time.
3. Law and morality usually overlap on major issues, but may differ on other matters.
4. Murder is an example of an overlap. It is both legally and morally wrong. However, even on this major issue there are groups who believe that euthanasia should be allowed and legally it has been ruled that the withdrawal of sustenance from a person in a persistent vegetative state is not murder (*Airedale NHS Trust v Bland* (1993)).

5. Law and morality diverge on many issues. For example:
- abortion is legal under the Abortion Act 1967, but some groups believe it is morally wrong;
- smoking cannabis is legally wrong but many people believe it is not morally wrong.

6. Whether law and morality should be the same is a question that is debated. Positivists such as Hart and Kelsen state that law and morality are essentially separate, but proponents of the natural law theory (based on the theories of Aristotle and St Thomas Aquinas) believe that law and morality should coincide.

1.1.3 A legal system

Professor Hart gave five factors which he thought had to co-exist to create a legal system. These are:

a) rules that forbid certain conduct and rules that compel certain conduct on pain of sanctions;

b) rules requiring people to compensate those whom they injure;

c) rules stating what needs to be done in certain 'mechanical' areas of law, such as making a contract or making a will;

d) a system of courts to determine what the rules are, whether they have been broken and what the appropriate sanction is;

e) a body whose responsibility it is to make rules and amend or repeal them when necessary.

1.2 CLASSIFICATION OF LAW

It is possible to classify law in many ways. For a law student the most important ways are by:
- the type of law (i.e. the matters that the law is regulating);
- the source from which it comes; this affects the status of the law.

1.2.1 Classification by types of law

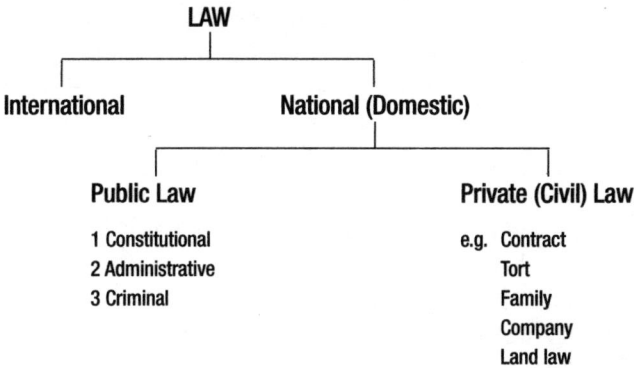

1. Law can be classified as international or national (domestic).
2. International law can be divided into public international law, which governs relationships between countries, and private international law, which governs which country's law should apply to individuals where there are links with at least two different countries. For example, which country's law should govern who inherits on a person's death.
3. National law can also be divided into public law and private law. Public law involves the State in some way, while private (civil) law controls the relationships between individuals.
4. National public law can be divided into:
  ● constitutional law;
  ● administrative law;
  ● criminal law.
5. National private law can be divided into many categories including contract, tort, family law, company law and land law.

1.2.2 Classification by source

1. European Union law is that which emanates from the Institutions of the EU. This can overrule national law (*R v Secretary of State for Transport ex parte Factortame* (1991)).

2. Statutory law is that made by an Act of Parliament, e.g. Access to Justice Act 1999. Apart from EU law, statutory law is sovereign and cannot be challenged by the courts.

3. Regulatory law is secondary law made by delegated legislation.

4. Common law is law made by the decisions of the judges. It is also referred to as case law.

5. Equity law is law created by the Chancery courts under the Lord Chancellor to 'fill the gaps' in the common law. Although equity prevails over common law, equitable remedies are discretionary.

1.2.3 Different meanings of common law

The phrase common law is used in a number of ways, so it is important to be aware of the context in which it is used.

Different meanings	Distinguishes it from
Law developed by judges in the eleventh and twelfth centuries to form a 'common' law for the whole country	The local laws used prior to the Norman conquest
Judge-made law developed through judicial precedent	Laws made by a legislative body such as Acts of Parliament (statutory law)
The law operated in the common law courts before the reorganisation of the court structure in 1873–75	Equity – decisions of the Chancery courts
Common law systems – those following the English case-based system (mainly US and Commonwealth countries)	Civil law systems – those operated in European countries influenced by Roman law and which are largely code based

1.3 DISTINCTIONS BETWEEN CIVIL AND CRIMINAL LAW

Civil and criminal law have separate functions and operate in different courts. It is important to understand the differences.

	Civil	Criminal
Purpose	• Regulates relationships between individuals • Dispute settlement • Enforcement of rights	• Prevention of certain types of conduct • Enforcement of behaviour • Punishment of offenders
Courts	High Court County Court	Crown Court Magistrates' Court
Burden of proof	Balance of probability	Beyond reasonable doubt
Outcomes of cases	Liability decided Civil remedy awarded e.g. • damages • injunction • declaration	Guilt or innocence decided Sentence imposed e.g. • imprisonment • community penalty • fine
Terminology	Claimant/defendant Making a claim (suing defendant) Finding of liability	Prosecution/defendant Charging defendant Finding of guilt

However, note that in some areas the distinction between civil and criminal law can be blurred.

1. Contempt of court in a civil case may lead to a prison sentence.
2. Orders such as antisocial behaviour orders (s1 Crime and Disorder Act 1998) are initially civil orders but, if broken, become criminal cases.

Doctrine of precedent
- *Stare decisis*
- Like cases treated alike
- Courts bound by those above them in hierarchy
- Appellate courts normally follow own past decisions
- Only *ratio decidendi* binding
- Need good law reports

Precedent in practice
- Original precedent
- Binding precedent
- Persuasive precedent
- *Ratio* and *obiter*
- Distinguishing
- Overruling
- Reversing

JUDICIAL

Hierarchy of courts
- European Court of Justice
- House of Lords
- Court of Appeal
- Divisional Courts
- High Court
- Inferior courts

Advantages
- Similar cases treated alike
- Certainty
- Law can develop
- Case illustrations of law

Disadvantages
- Can lead to injustice
- Too rigid
- Slow – has to wait for relevant case
- Complex – too detailed

2.1 THE DOCTRINE OF PRECEDENT

2.1.1 Stare decisis

1. It is a fundamental principle that like cases should be treated alike.
2. The Latin maxim *stare decisis* (stand by decisions of past cases) is the basis of the doctrine of precedent.

3. Precedent, as operated in the English legal system, requires that in certain circumstances a decision on a legal point made in an earlier case MUST be followed.

4. The doctrine is that:

- all courts are bound to follow decisions made by courts above them in the hierarchy; and
- appellate courts are normally bound by their own past decisions.

5. An extreme example of this was seen following the decision in *Re Schweppes Ltd's Agreement* (1965), in which one judge in the Court of Appeal dissented. Later on the same day, when the same point of law was involved in a second case (*Re Automatic Telephone and Electric Co. Ltd's Agreement* (1965)), that judge said he was now bound to follow the earlier decision.

2.1.2 Original precedent

1. Where there is no previous decision on a point of law that has to be decided by a court, then the decision made in that case on that point of law is an original precedent.

2. Usually, when faced with the situation of having to form an original precedent, the court will reason by analogy. Cases that are nearest to it in principle will be considered, though they are not binding. If there is any parallel, the court may decide that the same type of principle should apply (*Hunter and others v Canary Wharf Ltd and London Dockland Development Corporation* (1995)).

3. Such decisions used to be considered a declaratory precedent, i.e. the judges in the case merely declared what the law had always been, although this was the first time it had had to be decided. Supporters of this theory believed that judges did not create new law when making a decision; they merely declared what the law had always been. It is now accepted that judges do create law.

4. However, the declaratory theory still has relevance because a decision has a retrospective effect on the law (*Kleinwort Benson Ltd v Lincoln City Council* (1998)).

2.1.3 Binding and persuasive precedent

1. A past decision is binding only if:
   - the legal point involved is the same as the legal point in the case now being decided;
   - the facts of the present case are sufficiently similar to the previous case; and
   - the earlier decision was made by a court above the present court in the hierarchy, or by a court at the same level which is bound by its own past judgments; and
   - the point was argued in the case (*Kadhim v Brent London Borough Council* (2001)).
2. Only the ratio decidendi of the earlier case is binding (see 2.5 for details on *ratio decidendi* and *obiter dicta*).
3. A persuasive precedent is one which the court will consider and may be persuaded by, but which does not have to be followed.
4. Persuasive precedent comes from a variety of different sources. The main ones within the English legal system are:
   - *obiter dicta* statements by a higher ranking court, e.g. the Court of Appeal following *obiter dicta* of the House of Lords in *R v Howe* (1987) when deciding the case of *R v Gotts* (1992) on the non-availability of duress as to a charge of attempted murder;
   - a dissenting judgment;
   - ratios from decisions by courts lower in the hierarchy.
5. Decisions by courts outside the English legal system can also have a persuasive effect on English courts. The main ones of these are:
   - the Judicial Committee of the Privy Council;
   - the European Court of Human Rights (s2 Human Rights Act 1998);
   - courts in other countries, especially Commonwealth countries or countries with a common law system.

2.1.4 Law reporting

For a system of precedent to operate effectively it is essential that the reasons for decisions of past cases are properly recorded.

1. The earliest law reports were the Year Books from 1282 to 1537.

2. From 1537 to 1863 various private law reports were used. These varied in quality.

3. Since 1863 the Incorporated Council of Law Reporting has produced the official law reports.

4. There are also other well recognised series, especially the Weekly Law Reports and the All England Law Reports.

5. Since 1980 computerised law reports have been available through the LEXIS system.

6. Now, judgments of the House of Lords and the Court of Appeal are available on the Internet.

7. Before the use of the Internet only about 70% of House of Lords cases were reported and less than a quarter of the Court of Appeal cases were reported. Unreported cases can only be cited in court with the permission of the court (*Roberts Petroleum v Bernard Kenny Ltd* (1983)).

2.2 HIERARCHY OF THE COURTS

1. a) Where a point of European law is involved, the decisions of the European Court of Justice are binding on all courts in England and Wales.

b) The European Court of Justice does not have to follow its own past decisions. This is in accordance with the more flexible approach to precedent in European countries that have civil codes.

2. a) The House of Lords is the highest court in the UK and its decisions must be followed by all other courts in England and Wales.

b) The House of Lords will normally regard its own past decisions as binding, but will depart from them 'when it appears right to do so' (Practice Statement 1966; see 2.3 for further detail).

3. a)   The Court of Appeal has to follow decisions of the House of Lords (*Broome v Cassell & Co* (1971), *Miliangos v George Frank (Textiles) Ltd* (1976)).

   b)   The Court of Appeal (Civil Division) is bound to follow past decisions of its own (*Young v Bristol Aeroplane Co Ltd* (1944); see 2.4 for further detail).

   c)   The Court of Appeal (Criminal Division) will normally follow its own past decisions, but has flexibility to depart from a decision where the liberty of a person is involved (*R v Taylor* (1950); see 2.4 for further detail).

4. a)   Divisional courts must follow House of Lords and Court of Appeal decisions.

   b)   Divisional courts are normally bound by their own past decisions (*Huddersfield Police Authority v Watson* (1947)).

5. a)   The High Court must follow House of Lords, Court of Appeal and Divisional Court decisions.

   b)   The High Court does not usually have to follow past decisions of its own. However, where there are conflicting past decisions, 'the later decision is to be preferred if it is reached after full consideration of the earlier decisions' (*Colchester Estates v Carlton Industries* (1984)).

6. Inferior courts (Crown Court, County Court, Magistrates' Court) do not create precedents and must follow decisions of all the above courts.

2.3 THE HOUSE OF LORDS AND THE PRACTICE STATEMENT

2.3.1 The need for the Practice Statement

1. From the middle of the nineteenth century the House of Lords generally regarded themselves as bound by their own past decisions (*Beamish v Beamish* (1861)), but it was not until *London Tramways v London County Council* (1898) that this rule became completely fixed.

2. The reason for following their own past decisions was that it was in the public interest for there to be certainty in the law and to prevent the same point being re-argued.

3. The ruling in *London Tramways v London County Council* had the effect of making the law too rigid.

4. In 1966 the Lord Chancellor issued the Practice Statement giving the House of Lords flexibility to depart from past decisions. The Statement said that former decisions would normally be treated as binding, but the Lords could 'depart from a previous decision when it appears right to do so'.

5. The Statement recognised that 'too rigid adherence to precedent may lead to an injustice in a particular case and also unduly restrict the proper development of the law'.

6. However, the Statement stressed the need for certainty, especially in the criminal law, and the danger of disturbing retrospectively the basis on which contracts, settlements of property and fiscal arrangements had been entered into.

2.3.2 The use of the Practice Statement

1. The Lords did not rush to use the Practice Statement. The first use was in *Conway v Rimmer* (1968), which overruled *Duncan v Cammell Laird & Co* (1942) on a technical point.

2. The first major use was in *Herrington v British Railways Board* (1972), when the House of Lords overruled (or modified) the decision in *Addie & Sons v Dumbreck* (1929) on the liability of an occupier or premises to a child trespasser.

3. However, in the same year (1972) the Lords refused to use the Practice Statement in *Jones v Secretary of State for Social Services*, even though four of the seven judges believed the earlier case of *Re Dowling* (1967) to be wrongly decided.

4. The first use of the Practice Statement in a criminal case was in *R v Shivpuri* (1986) on attempts to do the impossible.

5. Since the mid 1980s the Statement has been used a little more. For example, in civil cases it was used in:

- *Murphy Brentwood District Council* (1991) to overrule the decision in *Anns v London Borough of Merton* (1978);
- *Pepper v Hart* (1993) to overrule *Davis v Johnson* (1979) on the use of Hansard as an extrinsic aid to interpretation of statutes.

In criminal cases it has been used in:

- *R v Howe* (1987) to overrule *DPP for Northern Ireland v Lynch* (1975) on the availability of the defence of duress to murder charge;
- *R v R* (1991) (marital rape);
- *R v Adomako* (1994), which overruled *R v Seymour* (1983) on the test for recklessness in manslaughter.

6. However, there are also many examples of refusal to use the Practice Statement.

2.4 THE POSITION OF THE COURT OF APPEAL

> Must follow decisions of the House of Lords (*Broome v Cassell, Miliangos*).
> Possible exceptions where a House of Lords' decision:
> - has been overruled by the European Court of Justice; or
> - is incompatible with the European Convention on Human Rights.

COURT OF APPEAL

CIVIL DIVISION

> Must follow own past decisions (*Davis v Johnson*).
> Exceptions in *Young's* case:
> - conflicting decisions;
> - impliedly overruled by House of Lords;
> - *per incuriam.*

CRIMINAL DIVISION

> Normally follows own past decisions.
> Same exceptions in *Young's case* apply.
> Also will not follow where law has been misapplied or misunderstood (*Gould*).

1. The Court of Appeal is bound to follow decisions of the European Court of Justice and the House of Lords.
2. In the 1970s there was a challenge (mainly by Lord Denning) to the rule that the Court of Appeal must follow House of Lords' decisions.
3. In *Broome v Cassell & Co* (1971) the Court of Appeal refused to follow *Rookes v Barnard* (1964) on the circumstances in which exemplary damages could be awarded. When *Broome v Cassell* was appealed to the House of Lords, the Law Lords reminded the Court of Appeal that it was 'necessary for each lower tier, including the Court of Appeal, to accept loyally the decisions of the higher tiers'.
4. In the cases of *Schorsch Meier GmbH v Henning* (1975) and *Miliangos v George Frank (Textiles) Ltd* (1976) the Court of Appeal refused to follow the House of Lords' decision in *Havana Railways* (1961) that damages could only be awarded in sterling. On the appeal of *Miliangos* to the House of Lords, the judges stated that 'the Court of Appeal is absolutely bound by a decision of the House of Lords'.
5. Since *Miliangos* there has been no further challenge to this basic principle of judicial precedent, except:
   * where a decision of the House of Lords is not compatible with the European Convention on Human Rights (*Director General of Fair Trading v The Proprietary Association of Great Britain* (2001));
   * a decision of the House of Lords has been subsequently overruled by the European Court of Justice.

2.4.1 Court of Appeal (Civil Division) and its own past decisions

1. The divisions do not bind each other.
2. The Civil Division must follow its own past decisions, unless they come within the exceptions in *Young v Bristol Aeroplane Co Ltd* (1944).

3. These exceptions are:
- the court is entitled to decide which of two conflicting past decision of its own it will follow;
- the court must refuse to follow a decision of its own which, though not expressly overruled, cannot stand with a decision of the House of Lords;
- the court is not bound to follow a decision of its own if it is satisfied that the decision was given *per incuriam.*

4. There is possibly another exception in interlocutory cases where an earlier decision made by a two-judge court can be overruled by a later three-judge court (*Boys v Chaplin* (1968)).

5. After 1966 Lord Denning argued that the principle of the Practice Statement should apply to the Court of Appeal, so that it would not be bound by its own past decisions. His main ground for the Court of Appeal was effectively the last appellate court in the vast majority of cases.

6. In *Davis v Johnson* (1979) the Court of Appeal refused to follow a past decision of its own made only a few days earlier. However, on appeal to the House of Lords, the Law Lords 'unequivocally and unanimously' re-affirmed the rule in *Young v Bristol Aeroplane.*

7. Since *Davis v Johnson* there has been no challenge by the Court of Appeal to the rule in *Young v Bristol Aeroplane.*

8. However, the Court of Appeal has used the *per incuriam* exception on some occasions (*Williams v Fawcett* (1985), *Rakhit v Carty* (1990)).

2.4.2 Court of Appeal (Criminal Division) and its own past decisions

1. a) In *R v Taylor* (1950) the Court of Criminal Appeal (the predecessor of the Court of Appeal (Criminal Division)) took the view that the exceptions that applied in civil cases 'ought not to be the only ones applied' in criminal cases.

b) The court held that as the liberty of the subject was involved, an earlier decision should not be followed where law has been misapplied or misunderstood.

2. In *R v Gould* (1968) the newly created Court of Appeal (Criminal Division) held that this same flexibility still applied.

3. In *R v Spencer* (1985) the Criminal Division stated that there was no difference between it and the Civil Division in respect of being bound by past decisions, save that when the liberty of the subject is at stake it might decline to follow one of its own decisions.

4. Where there are conflicting past decisions, the Criminal Division will prefer the one which favours the defendant (*R v Jenkins* (1983)).

2.5 RATIO AND OBITER

1. In a judgment there are several elements. There will always be:
   - findings of material facts;
   - statements of the principles of law;
   - the decision based on these two.

2. Only the principles of law that are essential to the decision are the *ratio decidendi*.

3. Statements of principles of law that are not relevant to the decision are *obiter dicta*.

4. Cross defines *ratio decidendi* as 'any rule expressly or impliedly treated by the judge as a necessary step in reaching his conclusion'.

5. Zander defines *ratio decidendi* as 'a proposition of law which decides the case, in the light or in the context of the material facts'.

6. Discovering the *ratio decidendi* of a case is not always easy for many reasons:
   - it is hardly ever stated expressly;
   - in appellate courts there may be more than one judgment with different *ratios*;
   - in extreme cases it may even be impossible to find the ratio (*Central Asbestos Co Ltd v Dodd* (1973)).

7. Although the *ratio* is given in the judgment of the first case, it is to a great extent determined by the court in a later case. It may be enlarged by being applied to a wider situation, or restricted by being confined to a narrow scope.
8. *Obiter dicta* can be persuasive (*High Trees Case* (1947)).

2.6 DISTINGUISHING

1. Where a judge considers the material facts of the present case are sufficiently different from an earlier case, he is distinguishing the case and may refuse to follow the earlier decision (*Merritt v Merritt* (1971), *Balfour v Balfour* (1919)).
2. Distinguishing is a major factor in allowing the doctrine of precedent to remain flexible.
3. Decisions that are questionable or unpopular may be restricted to a narrow area by distinguishing.

2.7 ADVANTAGES AND DISADVANTAGES OF PRECEDENT

It is important to realise that for nearly all the factors that can be given as an advantage there is also a disadvantage.

2.7.1 Advantages

1. It serves the interests of justice and fairness as similar cases are seen to be treated in a similar way.
2. It creates certainty in the law and allows lawyers to advise clients on the probable outcome of a case.
3. There is opportunity for the law to develop and change with society (*Herrington v British Railways Board* (1972)).
4. As decisions are based on real cases there are practical illustrations of the law.
5. It is a time-saving device, as for most situations there is an existing solution.

2.7.2 Disadvantages

1. The doctrine as applied in the English Legal System is too rigid. This mainly stems from two factors:
   - the House of Lords is reluctant to use the Practice Statement; and
   - the Court of Appeal is bound to follow decisions of the House of Lords.
2. This rigidity can create injustice in an individual case.
3. The law is slow to develop; it is recognised that areas of law are unclear and in need of reform, but changes cannot be made unless a case on the particular point of law comes before the court.
4. The law is complex, with too many fine distinctions.
5. The large number of reported cases make it difficult to find the relevant law.

2.8 THE JUDICIAL ROLE IN PRECEDENT

1. Large areas of law have been developed by the judges, for example, rules on formation of contracts, the tort of negligence, the meaning of intention in criminal law.
2. The right of judges to create and/or reform law is unconstitutional as judges are not our elected law-makers.
3. The development of the law can depend on whether the judge is an active or passive law-maker.
4. Active law-making can be seen in *R v R* (1991), where the House of Lords ruled that there was a crime of marital rape.
5. Passive law-making is illustrated by *C v DPP* (1995), where the House of Lords refused to change a common law presumption about the criminal responsibility of children under the age of 14, stating that it was for Parliament to make such changes.

Acts of Parliament

- Pressure for legislation
- Consultation
- Green and White Papers
- Drafting process
- Passage through Parliament
- Coming into force

Delegated legislation

- Types
  a) Orders in Council
  b) Statutory instruments
  c) Bylaws
- Need for delegated legislation
- Control by Parliament
- Control by the courts

LEGISLATION

Statutory interpretation

- Literal v purposive approach
- Literal, Golden and Mischief rules
- Intrinsic and extrinsic aids
- Rules of language
- Presumptions

3.1 ACTS OF PARLIAMENT

About 70 to 80 Acts of Parliament are passed each year. In addition there is a considerable amount of delegated legislation each year, including over 3000 statutory instruments. If a legislative provision is not clear then the judges have to interpret it in order to apply it.

3.1.1 Pre-Parliamentary process and consultation

1. Pressure for new laws comes from a variety of sources. The main ones are:
   - Government policy;
   - EU Law;
   - Law Commission reports;
   - reports by other commissions or committees;
   - pressure groups.
2. The Government sets out its legislative programme for the parliamentary session in the Queen's Speech at the opening of Parliament.
3. Usually the government department responsible for the projected legislation will decide whether to consult prior to issuing a Green Paper.
4. *Making the Law* (1992), a Report by the Hansard Society, emphasised the need for consultation. It pointed out that the lack of consultation could lead to last-minute changes in Bills as they went through Parliament, as happened with the Broadcasting Bill 1989.
5. Consultation has become more common in recent years.
6. The Law Commission has a duty to review areas of law and will research and consult before drawing up proposals for reform.
7. Some Bills may be the result of reports by other committees or commissions, which will have heard evidence about the issues concerned.

3.1.2 Green and White Papers

1. A Green Paper sets out the tentative proposals for changes to the law and invites comments.
2. Green papers were first used in 1967 and are now usually used as part of the legislative process.
3. A White Paper is a firm proposal for a new law. Sometimes there may be a draft Bill annexed to the White Paper.

3.1.3 The drafting process

1. A draft Act is called a Bill.
2. The vast majority of Bills are introduced by the Government of the day. These Government Bills are drafted by parliamentary counsel to the Treasury.
3. The Government department responsible for the legislation will give detailed instructions to the parliamentary counsel.
4. The Renton Committee in *Preparation of Legislation* (1975) criticised the quality of draftsmanship. The four main criticisms were:
   - the language used in statutes was obscure and complex;
   - over-elaboration in an effort to obtain certainty;
   - illogical and unhelpful structure;
   - amendment of previous acts by later acts making it difficult to discover the current law.
5. Since 1998 there must be a written statement that the Bill is compatible with the European Convention on Human Rights. Alternatively, the Government can say that no such statement could be made but they wish to proceed with the Bill.

3.2 THE PROCESS IN PARLIAMENT

Each Bill goes through a number of stages before it becomes an Act. If the Bill is voted against at the First Reading, Second Reading or Third Reading in either House then it does not become law.

3.2.1 Types of Bill

1. Government Bill – one introduced by the Government through the relevant Minister; such a Bill will almost always become law as the Government has a majority in the House of Commons.
2. Public Bill – one which relates to matters that affect the general public; most Government Bills will be public Bills.
3. Private Bill – one which relates to the powers and interests of certain private individuals or institutions (e.g. University College London Act 1996). The procedure for a private Bill is slightly different to that for a public Bill, with the Committee stage being the most important aspect, while the Second and Third Readings are more of a formality.
4. Hybrid Bill – one with features of both a public and a private Bill (e.g. Channel Tunnel Bill 1986–87).
5. Private Members' Bill – one which is introduced by a backbench MP. There are three ways in which this can be done:
   - drawing a position in the ballot held for each Parliamentary session;
   - under Standing Order No 39;
   - under the ten-minute rule (Standing Order No 10).
   The time in Parliament for Private Members' Bills is very restricted. Unless the Bill is supported by the Government, it has only a small chance of becoming law.
6. Consolidation Bill – one bringing together the provisions from a number of previous Acts without altering the law.

3.2.2 Passing a Bill

A Bill may be started in either the House of Commons or the House of Lords, but it has to go through the same procedure in each House and pass all stages of the legislative process to become law.

1. First Reading – a formality at which the title of the Bill is read out.

2. Second Reading – the main debate on the principles of the Bill.
3. Committee Stage – a consideration of each clause of the Bill.
4. Report stage – a report to the whole House of amendments proposed by the Committee stage.
5. Third Reading – the final vote on the Bill; there will be a further debate about the Bill only if at least six members request it.
6. The other house – if the Bill started in the House of Commons, then the above five stages are carried out in the House of Lords, and vice versa.
7. Royal Assent – a formal assent to the Bill by the Monarch. The Bill is now an Act of Parliament.

3.2.3 The Parliament Acts 1911 and 1949

1. The House of Lords' power to prevent Bills from becoming law is limited by these Acts.
2. For a 'Money Bill' that has been passed by the House of Commons, the Government may choose to re-introduce that Bill after one month and, if it passes the House of Commons for a second time, it then becomes law.
3. For all other Bills the delay time is one year.
4. The House of Commons very rarely uses the power under the Parliament Acts (e.g. War Crimes Act 1991).
5. Where a Bill has been started in the House of Lords but has been voted against, it cannot be re-introduced.

3.2.4 Coming into force

1. An Act of Parliament comes into force on:
   - the commencement date (if any) given in the Act; or
   - if there is an 'appointed day' section, on the date set by the appropriate Government minister; or
   - if there is no indication in the Act, then it becomes law at midnight following the Royal Assent.

2. There is much criticism of the use of appointed day sections, where different parts of the Act may be brought into effect at different times. This makes it difficult to discover whether a certain provision is in force or not.
3. Some sections may never be brought into force, bringing into question why they were enacted in the first place.

3.3 ADVANTAGES OF STATUTE LAW OVER CASE LAW

1. There is the opportunity for consultation.
2. Law can be passed to avoid future problems.
3. The change to the law is usually prospective, thus not affecting existing contracts, etc. However, a few Acts have been made retrospective (War Damage Act 1965, War Crimes Act 1991).
4. The law is known in advance, rather than after the judgment in a case.
5. An Act can cover a wide range of points.
6. Statutory law supersedes common law.
7. It cannot be normally be challenged because of the sovereignty of Parliament.

3.4 PARLIAMENTARY SOVEREIGNTY

1. No challenge can normally be made to an Act of Parliament.
2. This is so even if the Act is unreasonable or if it was produced by fraud (*British Railways Board v Pickin* (1974)).
3. However, where an Act is in conflict with European Union legislation, then the EU law takes priority (*Factortame case* No 1 (1989) and No 2 (1991)).
4. Since 2000, where an Act of Parliament is incompatible with the European Convention on Human Rights the court may make a declaration of incompatibility. This does not invalidate the Act, it simply draws the Government's attention to the problem and the Government can choose whether not to amend the Act.

3.5 DELEGATED LEGISLATION

Delegated legislation is law made by a body other than Parliament, but with Parliament's authority. That authority is given in a parent or enabling Act.

3.5.1 Types of delegated legislation

1. Orders in Council – made by the Queen and Privy Council. These can be made when Parliament is not sitting under the Emergency Powers Act 1920. There is also power to give effect to EU law under the European Communities Act 1972.
2. Statutory instruments – made by Government ministers. This is the most used type of delegated legislation.
3. Local authority bylaws – made by local councils in respect of matters in their area.
4. Bylaws made by public corporations – made to regulate behaviour in such areas as London Underground.
5. Court rules – made by Court Rules Committees in respect of the various courts and their procedures.

3.5.2 Need for delegated legislation

1. There is a lack of Parliamentary time for considering all necessary regulations.
2. It allows more detail to be included than is possible in an Act of Parliament.
3. There is expertise for matters requiring technical knowledge.
4. There is local knowledge for local bylaws.
5. It allows more time for consultation.
6. It is easier to amend than an Act of Parliament

3.5.3 Control of delegated legislation

Parliamentary	Judicial
Enabling Act sets parameters	Can be challenged in the courts under the doctrine of *ultra vires*
Affirmative resolution requires Parliamentary vote	This can be: ● substantive or ● procedural
Negative resolution allows a debate to be requested	If found to be *ultra vires* the legislation can be declared void
Delegated Powers Scrutiny Committee reports to House of Lords	
Joint Select Committee reviews Statutory Instruments	
Ministers can be questioned	

1. Parliament sets the parameters for the delegated legislation in the enabling Act.
2. The House of Lords' Delegated Powers Scrutiny Committee (set up in 1993) considers whether the provisions of Bills give inappropriate delegated legislative power. It reports to the House of Lords before the Committee Stage on the Bill.
3. The Joint Select Committee on Statutory Instruments reviews all statutory instruments and draws the attention of both Houses of Parliament to points that need to be considered. The main reasons for referring a statutory instrument to Parliament are:
   ● it imposes a tax;
   ● it has retrospective effect;
   ● it has gone beyond the powers given in the enabling Act;
   ● it makes unusual or unexpected use of the powers;
   ● it is unclear or defective in some way.
4. A few statutory instruments have to be considered and approved by Parliament under the affirmative resolution procedure. The enabling Act specifies where this is required.

5. Most statutory instruments are subject to the negative resolution procedure. This means that they will become law within 40 days unless a debate is requested by an MP.
6. MPs may question the relevant minister in Parliament about proposed delegated legislation.
7. The courts can declare void any delegated legislation which goes beyond its powers under the doctrine of *ultra vires*. (See, for example, *R v Home Secretary, ex parte Fire Brigades* Union (1995), *R v Lord Chancellor, ex parte Witham* (1997)).
8. Delegated legislation can also be declared *ultra vires* because the correct procedures were not followed (*Aylesbury Mushroom case* (1972)).

3.5.4 Disadvantages of delegated legislation

1. It is undemocratic as most regulations are made by civil servants or other unelected people, except for local authority bylaws which are made by an elected council.
2. Henry VIII clauses can give power to delegated legislation to amend or repeal Acts of Parliament.
3. There is inadequate Parliamentary control.
4. There is a lack of publicity.
5. There are too many regulations through delegated legislation.

3.6 STATUTORY INTERPRETATION

A large percentage of cases heard by the House of Lords and the Court of Appeal (Civil Division) involve the meanings of words in a statute or delegated legislation.

3.6.1 Need for statutory interpretation

1. Words are an imperfect means of communication.
2. There may be ambiguity – words often have more than one meaning.
3. A broad term may have been used which is not clear (*Brock v DPP* (1993) on the meaning of 'type' in the Dangerous Dogs Act 1991).

4. There may have been a drafting error or omission.
5. New developments can lead to words not covering present-day situations (*Royal College of Nursing v DHSS* (1981)).

3.6.2 Approaches to statutory interpretation

There is a major debate as to whether judges should interpret legislation so as to give effect to the intention or purpose of that legislation (purposive approach), or whether judges should take the words at their literal meaning (literal approach).
1. The literal approach gives words their plain, ordinary, dictionary meaning.
2. The literal approach is preferred by 'conservative' judges who do not believe that a judge's role is to create law.
3. The purposive approach is a broader approach. Judges try to decide what Parliament was trying to achieve.
4. The purposive approach is the one favoured by activist or creative judges.
5. The European approach to interpretation is based on the purposive approach.

3.6.3 Rules of interpretation

The courts developed three 'rules': the literal rule, the golden rule and the mischief rule, for statutory interpretation. These rules have now largely been supersede by the literal versus purposive approach, but even so they are sometimes used.
1. Literal rule – this uses the plain, ordinary, literal, grammatical meaning of the words (*Whiteley v Chappell* (1868), *London and North Eastern Railway Co v Berriman* (1946), *Lees v Secretary of State for Social Services* (1985)).
   - Where words have a technical legal meaning then, under the literal rule, this will be used (*Fisher v Bell* (1960)).
   - 'If the words of an Act are clear, then you must follow them, even though they lead to a manifest absurdity' (Lord Esher in *R v Judge of the City of London Court* (1892)).

2. Golden rule – this is a modification of the literal rule, where the literal interpretation would lead to an absurdity. Zander has described this rule as 'an unpredictable safety-valve to permit the courts to escape from some of the more unpalatable effects of the literal rule'.

3. There are two ways in which the golden rule has operated in cases:
   - the narrow application, where words are capable of having more than one meaning, in which case the meaning that is least absurd should be used (*R v Allen* (1872));
   - the wider application, which is used to modify words to avoid an absurdity (*Adler v George* (1964)) or to avoid a repugnant situation (*Re Sigsworth* (1935)).

4. Mischief rule – this was first formulated in *Heydon's case* (1584). The court looks to see what gap or 'mischief' in the law the Act was passed to cover (*Smith v Hughes* (1960)).

3.6.4 Intrinsic aids

1. Intrinsic aids are those other parts of the Act which may help to make the meaning of the particular section clear. These are:
   - the long title and the short title;
   - the preamble, if any;
   - definition sections;
   - schedules;
   - headings before any section or groups of sections.

2. Marginal notes are not generally accepted as an intrinsic aid as they are not part of the Act as voted on by Parliament, but are added at the printing stage.

3.6.5 Extrinsic aids

1. These are matters outside the Act in question which may be considered by the courts. Extrinsic aids that are fully accepted are:
   - dictionaries;
   - historical setting;
   - previous Acts of Parliament;
   - earlier case law.

2. Reference to Hansard is now allowed, but only where:
- the legislation is ambiguous or obscure; and
- the material relied on consists of statements made by a minister or other promoter of the Bill; and
- the statements relied on are clear.

3. Where the court is interpreting law that was passed to give effect to an international convention or a European directive, then Hansard can be used more widely. The court may consider ministerial statements even if the statute does not appear to be ambiguous or obscure (*Three Rivers District Council and others v Bank of England (No 2)* (1996)).

4. Law reform reports by bodies such as the Law Commission may be considered, but only to discover the mischief or gap in the law which the legislation based on the report was designed to deal with (*Black Clawson case* (1975)).

5. International conventions and any *travaux preparatoire* material issued in relation to the convention may be considered when considering the meaning of English legislation based on the convention (*Fothergill v Monarch Airlines Ltd* (1980)).

3.6.6 Rules of language

These are rules to aid interpreting certain formats of words. If the particular format is not used then the rule has no relevance. The rules are:
- *ejusdem generis* – where a list of words is followed by general words, then the general words are limited to the same kind of items as those in the list (*Powell v Kempton Park Race Course* (1899));
- *expressio unius exclusio alterius* – the mention of one thing excludes another. Where there is a list of words which is not followed by general words then the Act applies only to the items in the list (*Tempest v Kilner* (1846));
- *noscitur a sociis* – a word is known by the company it keeps. Words must be looked at in their context (*Inland Revenue Commissioners v Frere* (1965)).

3.6.7 Presumptions

The courts will make certain presumptions about the law, but these are only a starting point. If the Act expressly or by implication states that the presumption will not apply, then it does not. The main presumptions are:

- against a change to the common law;
- that mens rea is required;
- the Crown is not bound unless the statute expressly says so;
- parliament did not intend to oust the jurisdiction of the courts;
- legislation does not apply retrospectively.

3.6.8 The European approach

1. The purposive approach to interpretation is favoured by most European legal systems. Consequently, the European Court of Justice takes this approach.
2. In *Henn and Derby v DPP* (1981) Lord Diplock contrasted this with the English courts' approach, saying the European Court of Justice 'seeks to give effect to what it perceives to be the spirit rather than the letter of the Treaties'.
3. The Treaty of Rome requires Member States to 'take all appropriate measures . . . to ensure the fulfilment of the obligations' under the Treaty. This encourages the courts in Member States to use the purposive approach.
4. Where a European Directive has been issued 'national courts are required to interpret their national law in the light of the wording and the purpose of the directive' (*von Colson v Land Nordrhein-Westfalen* (1984)).
5. As a result, when deciding points of law that involve European law, the English courts are using the purposive approach.
6. There has also been a gradual move towards a greater use of the purposive approach in other cases before the English courts (*Pepper v Hart* (1993)).

3.6.9 The judicial role in interpretation

1. Traditionalist judges favour the passive role in interpretation, believing that they should apply the law as shown by the words, and not 'fill in the gaps' in legislation.

2. This view was expressed by Viscount Dilhorne: 'If language is clear and explicit, the court must give effect to it, for in that case the words of the state speak for the intention of the legislature' (*Kammins Ballroom Co Ltd v Zenith Investments Ltd* (1970)).

3. Activist judges favour the purposive approach to interpretation and see their role as a more creative one.

4. Lord Denning was a major supporter of the activist role: 'We sit here to find out the intention of Parliament and carry it out, and we do this better by filling in the gaps and making sense of the enactment than by opening it up to destructive analysis' (*Magor and St Mellons RDC v Newport Corporation* (1950)).

5. This statement was criticised by Lord Simonds in the same case on appeal to the House of Lords, when he said it was 'a naked usurpation of the legislative function under the thin guise of interpretation'.

6. The decision in *Pepper v Hart* (1993) on the use of Hansard shows a move towards a more activist role. However, the limitations placed on the use of Hansard make it clear that the House of Lords is still not prepared to take too creative an approach to statutory interpretation.

CHAPTER 4

EUROPEAN UNION LAW

```
┌─────────────────────────────────────────┐
│              THE INSTITUTIONS             │
│  Council – government representatives     │
│  Commission – 20 independent commissioners│
│  Parliament – 626 directly elected MEPs   │
│  European Court of Justice – 15 judges    │
└─────────────────────────────────────────┘
                     ↑
            EUROPEAN UNION
                     ↓
┌─────────────────────────────────────────┐
│              SOURCES OF LAW               │
│      Treaties – directly applicable       │
│     Rgeulations – directly applicable     │
│    Directives – vertical direct effect    │
└─────────────────────────────────────────┘
                     ↓
┌─────────────────────────────────────────┐
│           EFFECT ON SOVEREIGNTY           │
│   EU law takes priority over national law │
│         Van Gend en Loos (1963)           │
│           Factortame (1990)               │
└─────────────────────────────────────────┘
```

The European Union (originally the European Economic
Community) was founded in 1957 with six members. The
United Kingdom joined in 1973 and Union membership now
stands at 15. There are negotiations over membership for
another 12 countries so that by 2005 the membership of the
Union could be 27.

The founding Treaty was the Treaty of Rome 1957 (the EC
Treaty). This has been added to and amended by subsequent
treaties and the numbering of the Articles was altered in 1999 by
the Treaty of Amsterdam.

4.1 THE INSTITUTIONS

4.1.1 The Council of the European Union

1. The Council is attended by a government representative of each member state who must be 'at ministerial level, authorised to commit the government of that Member State' (Article 203 Treaty of Rome).
2. The Presidency is held by each Member State in rotation for a period of six months.
3. The Council is the principal decision-making body of the Union.
4. Sensitive areas such as taxation and social security must be decided by a unanimous vote.
5. For most other matters decisions are made by a qualified majority on a weighted voting basis. Each state has a set number of votes based on its population size.
6. At the moment the UK, Germany, France and Italy have ten votes while the smallest state, Luxembourg, has two votes.
7. The Nice Summit agreed new weightings for when the Union expands in 2005.

4.1.2 The Commission

1. There are 20 Commissioners who are appointed for a five-year term, with two each from the UK, Germany, France, Italy and Spain and one from the other Member States.
2. Commissioners must act in the best interests of the Union. They are supposed to be independent of their national origin and, in the performance of their duties, must 'neither seek nor take instructions from any government or from any other body' (Article 213(2) Treaty of Rome).
3. The Commission is the motive force behind Union policy. It proposes policies and presents drafts of legislation to the Council for consideration by the Council.
4. The Commission is also the 'guardian of the treaties' and ensures that treaty provisions and other measures are implemented by Member States.

5. The Commission may refer an infringement by a member state to the European Court of Justice (Article 226 Treaty of Rome).
6. It also has investigative powers over alleged infringements (Article 213 Treaty of Rome).
7. It is responsible for the administration of the Union and has executive powers to implement the Union's budget.

4.1.3 The Parliament

1. Members of the Parliament are elected by the citizens of the Member States. Elections take place once every five years. There is a total of 626 MEPs, with the UK having 87.
2. The Parliament has no direct law-making authority. Its role is to discuss proposals and put questions to the Council and the Commission.
3. However, it has some important control functions. It has power to dismiss the Commission by passing a vote of censure (Article 201 Treaty of Rome). In 1999 the entire Commission resigned to forestall such a censure vote.
4. The Parliament has some power over the budget, especially on non-necessary expenditure.
5. Under Article 195 (Treaty of Rome) the Parliament may appoint an Ombudsman to receive complaints of maladminstration by the Union institutions. The first Ombudsman was appointed in 1995.

4.1.4 Other representative bodies

1. The Economic and Social Committee advises the Commission and the Council on economic matters.
2. It comprises 'representatives of the various categories of economic and social activity, in particular, representatives of producers, farmers, carriers, workers, dealers, craftsmen, professional occupations and representatives of the general public' (Article 257 Treaty of Rome).

3. The Committee of the Regions advises the Commission and the Council on regional matters.

4.1.5 The European Court of Justice

1. The function of the court is 'to ensure that in the interpretation and application of the Treaty the law is observed' (Article 220 Treaty of Rome).

2. There are 15 judges who are appointed from those eligible for appointment to the highest judicial posts in their own country (Article 222 Treaty of Rome).

3. The court is assisted by eight Advocates-General whose task is to research all the legal points involved and 'to present publicly, with complete impartiality and independence, reasoned conclusions on cases submitted to the Court of Justice with a view to assisting the latter in the performance of its duties' (Article 223 Treaty of Rome).

4. The court has wide jurisdiction over Union law. It hears cases brought by the institutions, Member States or individuals alleging a breach of Union law. A main area here is the role of the Commission in bringing cases against Member States.

5. It also hears cases referred by courts in any Member State for a preliminary ruling on a point of Union law (Article 234 Treaty of Rome).

6. Such referrals are mandatory where no further appeal is possible in the Member State's court system and discretionary from any other court.

7. The European Court of Justice operates in a different way to English courts. The main differences are:
- cases are presented on paper with only limited oral argument;
- an Advocate-General is used to present an independent view of the law;
- judgments are always given in a written form as the decision of the whole court; it is never revealed if there were any dissenting judges;
- the court is not bound by its own previous decisions;

● the court uses the purposive approach to interpretation.

4.2 SOURCES OF LAW

Source	Effect	Cases
Treaties	Directly applicable	*van Duyn* (1974)
	Have both vertical and horizontal direct effect	*Macarthys v Smith* (1980)
Regulations A 249	Directly applicable	*Re Tachographs* (1979)
	Have both vertical and horizontal direct effect	*Leonesio* (1972)
Directives A 249	Have vertical direct effect	*Marshall* (1986)
	Do *not* have horizontal direct effect	*Duke v GEC* (1988)
	Can sue State under Francovitch principle	*Francovitch* (1991)
Recommendations and opinions A 249	'Soft' law	*Grimaldi* (1989)
	Must be taken into consideration when interpreting law	

Effect of the different sources of law

4.2.1 Treaties

1. Treaties are the primary source of European Union law.
2. All treaties are 'without further enactment to be given legal effect or used in the United Kingdom' (s2(1) European Communities Act 1972).
3. Treaties are therefore directly applicable and, where a treaty creates individual rights, then those rights can be relied on by an individual (*Van Duyn v Home Office* (1974), *Macarthys Ltd v Smith* (1980)).

4.2.2 Regulations

1. Regulations are issued under Article 249 of the Treaty of Rome.
2. This makes the effect of regulations as 'binding in every respect and directly applicable in each Member State'.
3. Member States must enforce regulations; they have no choice over whether to bringing them into effect (*Commission v UK: Re Tachographs* (1979)).
4. Regulations have vertical and horizontal effect. This means that citizens may rely on them both against the state and against other private individuals or bodies (*Leonesio v Ministero dell' Agricoltura* (1972)).

4.2.3 Directives

1. Directives are issued under Article 249 of the Treaty of Rome.
2. Directives 'bind any Member State to which they are addressed as to the result to be achieved, while leaving to domestic agencies a competence as to form and means'.
3. They are issued with a time limit for implementation in the Member States. If a directive is not implemented it will have vertical direct effect when the time limit for implementation expires. So where the directive creates individual rights, those rights may be relied on against the State or an 'arm of the State' (*Marshall v Southampton and South West Hampshire Area Health Authority* (1986)).
4. The concept of an 'arm of the State' is a body that has been made responsible for providing a public service under the control of the State (*Foster v British Gas plc* (1990)).
5. However, directives that have not been implemented do not have horizontal direct effect. They cannot be relied on against private individuals or bodies (*Duke v GEC Reliance Ltd* (1988), *Dori v Recreb Srl* (1994)).
6. Where a directive has not been implemented, an individual who suffers loss as a result of the non-implementation may sue the State for their breach of Community law (*Francovitch*

v Italian Republic (1991)).

7. In *Dori v Recreb Srl* (1994) the European Court of Justice held that compensation would be payable where:
   * the purpose of the directive was to grant rights to individuals;
   * those rights could be identified from the directive;
   * there was a causal link between the breach of the State's obligations and the damage suffered.

8. In *R v HM Treasury, ex parte British Telecommunications plc* (1996) the court said that compensation would only be payable where the breach was sufficiently serious.

4.2.4 Recommendations and opinions

1. These are also issued under Article 249. Neither creates enforceable rights.

2. However, national courts are bound to take them into consideration when interpreting national law adopted to give effect to a recommendation (*Grimaldi v Fondes des Maladies Professionelles* (1989)).

3. This effect is known as 'soft law', as opposed to the 'hard law' effect of legislation with binding force.

4.3 EFFECT ON SOVEREIGNTY OF PARLIAMENT

4.3.1 Conflict between EU law and national law

1. In *Van Gend en Loos* (1963), where there was a conflict between the Treaty of Rome and an earlier Dutch law, the European Court of Justice said that 'the Member States have limited their sovereign rights, albeit within limited fields, and have created a body of law which binds both their nationals and themselves'.

2. In *Costa v ENEL* (1964) there was a conflict between a number of Treaty provisions and a later Italian law, which under Italian law would take priority. The European Court of

Justice held that 'The reception, within the laws of each member State, of provisions having a Community source . . . has as a corollary the impossibility, for the Member State, to give preference to a unilateral and subsequent measure . . .'.

3. In *Internationale Handelsgesellschaft mbH* (1970) the court held that an EU regulation that conflicted with the German constitution took precedence over the German law.

4. In *Simmenthal SpA (No 2)* (1979) the court stated that national courts are under a duty to give full effect to the provisions of EU law and, if necessary, should refuse to apply national laws that conflict with EU law.

4.3.2 Sovereignty of Parliament

1. The fact that EU takes precedence over national law means that while the UK is a member of the Union, Parliament is no longer the supreme law-maker.

2. This was stressed when the validity of the Merchant Shipping Act 1988 was challenged as it conflicted with the Treaty of Rome (*R v Secretary of State for Transport, ex parte Factortame* (1990)).

3. Domestic courts are under a duty to apply EU law in preference to national law.

CHAPTER 5

LAW REFORM

Need for law reform
- Law made piecemeal
- Many obsolete statutes
- Low priority for Parliament
- Judges limited in powers to reform
- No Ministry of Justice

Law Commission
- Established by Law Commission Act 1965
- Full-time
- Five commissioners
- Researches/consults
- Report + draft bill
- Many reforms
- Failure to codify
- 70% of reports enacted

LAW REFORM

Other law reform bodies
- Law Reform Committee
- Criminal Law Revision Committee
- Royal Commissions, e.g. Phillip Commission
- Various *ad hoc* committees and reviews, e.g. Woolf Review

5.1 THE NEED FOR LAW REFORM

1. English law has developed in a piecemeal fashion; there is no code of law, unlike many European countries.
2. Judges can only reform law on individual points that come before the courts as cases arise (e.g. *R v R* (1991), making marital rape an offence).
3. Parliament has many other functions, and reform of 'lawyers' law' in particular often takes a low priority (e.g. the failure to implement the Draft Code of Criminal law).
4. There are many statutes that have become obsolete, but which have never been repealed.
5. Before 1965 there were only part-time law reform bodies, such as the Law Reform Committee and the Criminal Law Revision Committee.
6. It was felt that there was a need for a full-time law reform body, so the Law Commission was created.

5.2 LAW COMMISSION

5.2.1 Composition and working

1. This was established by the Law Commissions Act 1965.
2. It is a full-time body with a chairman, who is a High Court judge seconded to the Law Commission for a term of three years, and four other Law Commissioners.
3. Its role is:
   - to systematically develop and reform the law;
   - to simplify and modernise the law;
   - to codify the law;
   - to eliminate anomalies;
   - to repeal obsolete and unnecessary enactments.
4. The Lord Chancellor may refer topics to the Law Commission, but most topics are selected by the Commission itself, which then seeks Governmental approval to draft a report on the topic.

5. The area of law is researched, then a consultation paper is published setting out the current law, the problems with it and possible options for reform.

6. After consultation, the Commission will draw up positive proposals for reform. These will be presented in a report which will also set out the research that led to the conclusions.

7. A draft Bill may be attached to the report showing precisely how the law should be reformed.

5.2.2 Implementation of reports

1. Overall about 70% of the Law Commission's reports have eventually led to legislation.

2. However, the rate has not been consistent. In the first ten years 85% of reports were enacted by Parliament. In the next ten years only 50% became law. In 1990 not one proposal was made law.

3. In 1993 the Jellicoe procedure was introduced in order to speed up the adoption of law reform proposals. Under this a Special Standing Committee of the House of Lords heard evidence about proposals and considered the Bill in detail. This usually led to a quick passage through the remaining Parliamentary stages and, in 1993–94 13 Law Commission reports became law. This procedure has not been used recently.

4. The lack of Parliamentary commitment to law reform has been frequently been commented on by successive chairmen of the Law Commission in their annual reports.

5. A major area that has been ignored by Parliament is the reform of the criminal law. In 1985 a Draft Criminal Code was published by the Law Commission. No part of this has ever been implemented by Parliament.

5.2.3 Achievements of the Law Commission

1. Many Acts of Parliament have been enacted as the result of Law Commission reports.

2. Examples include:
* Unfair Contract Terms Act 1977;
* Occupiers Liability Act 1984;
* Law Reform (Year and a Day Rule) Act 1996;
* Contract (Rights of Third Parties) Act 1999.

3. The Law Commission has also 'tidied up' the statute book by the repeal of over 1,500 obsolete statutes.

5.3 OTHER LAW REFORM BODIES

1. The part-time Law Reform Committee still contributes to law reform of civil law (e.g. Latent Damage Act 1986) and is consulted by the Law Commission on certain areas, e.g. trust law.

2. The part-time Criminal Law Revision Committee sat from 1957 to 1987 and one of its main achievements was the reform of the law of theft and related offences in the Theft Act 1968.

3. Temporary commissions or committees are used to review one specific area of law or the legal system. These are often chaired by a judge, with the commission being referred to by the name of that judge. Some of their proposals may become law. Examples include:
* the Royal Commission on Police Procedure (Phillips Commission 1981), which led to the Police and Criminal Evidence Act 1984;
* the Royal Commission on Criminal Justice (Runciman Commission 1993), some of whose recommendations were implemented in the Criminal Appeal Act 1995 and the Criminal Procedure and Investigations Act 1996;
* the Woolf review of the civil justice system, which led to the Civil Procedure Rules 1999 and wide-ranging reform of the system.

CHAPTER 6

THE CIVIL JUSTICE SYSTEM

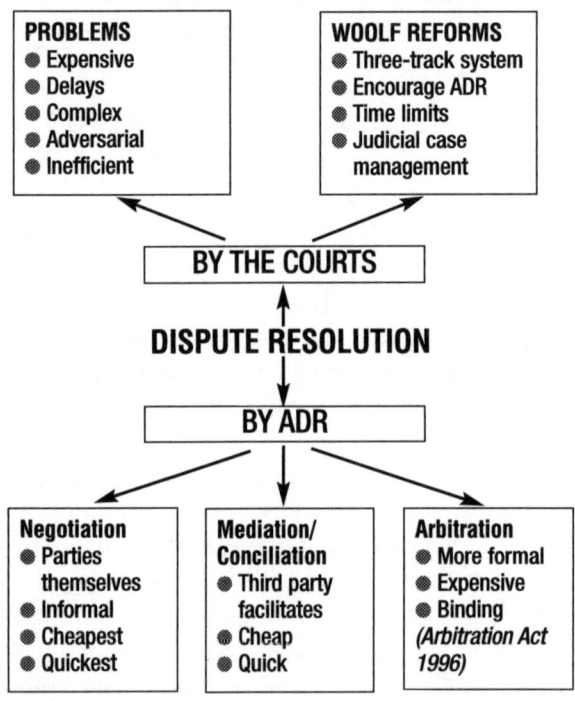

Civil justice has always been seen as too expensive and too complex, with long delays. In 1999 the Woolf Reforms of the civil justice system tried to address these problems.

6.1 THE COURT STRUCTURE

6.1.1 The three tracks

All cases that are defended are allocated to one of three tracks.
1. Small claims track – this is for most cases under £5000. Note that the normal limit for housing disrepair cases and personal

injury cases is £1000, while illegal eviction and harassment cases are excluded from the small claims track.

2. Fast track cases – these are claims for between £5000 and £15,000, although cases of this amount involving a complex point of law can be allocated to the multi-track.

3. Multi-track cases – these are claims over £15,000, or complex cases for less than this amount.

6.1.2 The civil courts

1. There are two civil courts that hear cases at first instance. These are the County Court and the High Court.

2. The County Court hears all small claims cases and all fast track cases. County Courts, which are designated as Civil Trial Centres, can also deal with multi-track cases above £15,000. However, unless the parties agree, cases above £50,000 in value are not usually tried in the County Court.

3. The High Court has three divisions.
   - Queen's Bench Division – for contract and tort claims; there are also special courts in the Commercial List, Technology and Construction List, and in the Admiralty Court.
   - Chancery Division – for disputes involving matters such as mortgages, trusts, copyright and patents; winding up of companies is dealt with by the Companies Court within this Division.
   - Family Division – for family-related disputes, wardship cases and cases relating to children under the Children Act 1989.

6.2 PROCEDURE IN OUTLINE

1. The Civil Procedure Rules 1999 sets out the rules for each stage of a case.

2. The overriding objective of the Rules is to enable the court to deal with cases justly by:
   - ensuring that the parties in any case are on an equal footing;

- dealing with cases in a way which is proportionate to the amount involved and the importance of the case.

3. Parties are encouraged to disclose the facts of their case prior to starting any court case. For some types of claim (e.g. personal injury) a pre-action protocol must be followed.

4. All claims for less than £15,000 must be started in the County Court. Claims for more than this amount can be started in either the High Court or the County Court, except personal injury claims for less than £50,000, which must be started in the County Court.

5. Most types of claim are started by issuing a Part 7 claim form. Particulars of a claim must be included on the claim form, or attached to it, or served separately within 14 days of the claim form being served.

6. There must also be a statement of truth as to the facts in the particulars of the claim.

7. The claim form and the particulars of the claim must be served on the defendant. This may be done by the court or the claimant and can be served personally, by post, by fax, by e-mail or other electronic means.

8. The defendant has 14 days in which to respond. A defendant may:
- pay the claim;
- admit or partly admit it;
- file an acknowledgement of service (but then must file a defence within another 14 days);
- file a defence.

9. A defence that just denies the claim is not sufficient; it should be more specific.

10. At any point before or after the commencement of proceedings, the defendant or the claimant may make a Part 36 offer (to settle) and payment.

6.2.1 Allocation of cases

1. When a defence is filed at court, an allocation questionnaire is sent to all parties. This helps the judge decide which track the case should be allocated to.
2. An allocation fee has to be paid at this stage, but not for claims under £1000.
3. If a party is dissatisfied with the allocation decision, an application can be made to the court for the claim to be re-allocated.

6.2.2 Small claims procedure

1. Cases are heard by a District Judge who will normally use an interventionist approach.
2. Cases are dealt with in a relatively informal way, although they are now heard in open court. Prior to the 1999 reforms small claims cases were heard in private.
3. The use of lawyers is discouraged because the winning party cannot recover the costs of using a lawyer from the losing side.
4. There may be a paper adjudication if the judge thinks it is appropriate and the parties agree.

6.2.3 Fast track cases

1. The concept of the fast track was described by Lord Woolf as 'intended to provide improved access to justice . . . by providing a strictly limited procedure designed to take cases to trial in a short but reasonable time-scale at a fixed cost'.
2. There are standard directions by the court for trial preparation.
3. There is a maximum delay of 30 weeks between directions and trial.
4. Normally only one expert witness is allowed and, if the parties cannot agree on an expert, the court has power to appoint one. The expert's evidence will be given in writing.
5. There are fixed costs for the advocate at the trial.

6.2.4 Multi-track cases

1. There is no standard procedure for pre-trial directions; the judge has flexibility to use a number of different approaches, including case management conferences and pre-trial reviews.
2. The aim is to identify the issues as early as possible and, where appropriate, try specific issues prior to the main trial. This is aimed at encouraging a settlement.
3. The number of expert witnesses is controlled by the court as the court's permission is needed for any party to use an expert to give evidence (oral or written).
4. All time limits are strictly enforced. An approximate date for the trial (a 'trial window') is given to the parties and the court is very unlikely to agree to any adjournment.

6.3 APPEALS

6.3.1 Appeal routes

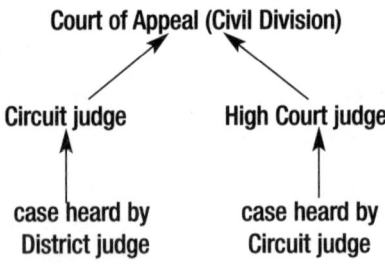

Appeals in small claims and fast track cases

1. Since 2000 appeals may be made in small claims cases under Rule 52 CPR; the route is for an appeal from a decision by a District judge to go to a Circuit judge. Appeals for small claims were introduced in order to comply with the European Convention on Human Rights.
2. Appeals for fast track cases depend on which level of judge heard the case. An appeal from a District judge goes to a Circuit judge; an appeal from a Circuit judge goes to a High Court judge.

3. A second appeal to the Court of Appeal (Civil Division) may only be made where the Court of Appeal considers that:
   a) the appeal would raise an important point of principle or practice; or
   b) there is some other compelling reason for the Court of Appeal to hear it (s55(1) Access to Justice Act 1999).

This has the effect that second appeals for small claims or fast track cases will become a rarity (*Tanfern Ltd v Cameron-Macdonald* (2000)).

House of Lords

↑

Court of Appeal (Civil Division)

↑

**All appeals from High Court
and
County Court multi-track cases**

Appeals in multi-track cases

4. Appeals from the final decision in a multi-track case heard in the County Court go to the Court of Appeal.
5. All appeals from decisions of the High Court go to the Court of Appeal. The exception to this is where an appeal is made direct to the House of Lords under the leapfrog procedure (Administration of Justice Act 1969).
6. In a multi-track case where there has been an appeal to the Court of Appeal, then a further appeal to the House of Lords is possible.

6.3.2 The approach to appeals

1. Permission to appeal is usually required; this can either be from the trial court or the relevant appeal court.
2. Permission will only be granted where the court considers:
   - that an appeal would have a real prospect of success; or
   - that there is some other compelling reason why the appeal should be heard.

3. The prospect of success must be realistic rather than fanciful (*Swain v Hillman* (1999)).

4. Permission to appeal is not required where the liberty of the individual is in issue, e.g. an appeal against a committal order.

5. Rule 52.11 states that an appeal will only be allowed (i.e. successful) where the decision of the lower court was wrong or where it was unjust because of a serious procedural or other irregularity.

6.4 COMMENT ON THE POST-WOOLF CIVIL SYSTEM

1. It is generally felt that the reforms are a qualified success.

2. The adversarial approach has been replaced by more co-operation between parties, and the use of ADR has increased.

3. The real issues of cases are being defined more quickly and this is leading to more cases settling and earlier settlements (rather than 'court door' settlements on the day of the trial).

4. The main problems are that:
   - the system is heavily front loaded, both in work to be done and in cost;
   - the new procedures, such as pre-action protocols, allocation questionnaires and case management conferences are more complex;
   - the rules on time limits are very strictly enforced, e.g. *Vinos v Marks and Spencer plc* (2000), where the claim was struck out because the claim form was served nine days after the expiry of the time.

6.5 ALTERNATIVE DISPUTE RESOLUTION

6.5.1 Negotiation

1. This is an informal approach between the parties themselves or their lawyers.
2. It is completely private and is the quickest and cheapest method of resolving a dispute.

6.5.2 Mediation/conciliation

1. Mediation is a process in which a neutral person (the mediator) helps the parties reach a compromise solution to their dispute. The mediator will discuss the position of each party with them and what outcomes they want from the dispute, but will not usually offer an opinion. The emphasis is on the parties themselves working out a solution.
2. Conciliation goes beyond mediation in that the mediator (or conciliator) has power to suggest grounds for compromise and the possible basis for a settlement.
3. There are a number of mediation/conciliation services, e.g. the Centre for Dispute Resolution.
4. ADR allows the parties to have control over the resolution process as they can withdraw at any time and a solution cannot be imposed on them – they must agree to it.
5. The process is preferred to court proceedings as it is:
   * cheaper;
   * quicker;
   * more informal;
   * allows business relations to remain more amicable between the parties.
6. The main disadvantage is that neither mediation or conciliation will necessarily lead to an agreement.

6.5.3 Arbitration

1. This the voluntary submission by the parties of their dispute to the judgment of an arbitrator (or panel of arbitrators) who is neutral.

2. The agreement to arbitrate is usually in writing, and written arbitration agreements are governed by the Arbitration Act 1996.

3. The agreement to go to arbitration can be made before a dispute arises (usually by a *Scott v Avery* clause in a contract) or after the dispute has arisen.

4. The agreement will either name an arbitrator or provide a method of choosing one. If the parties cannot agree on an arbitrator the court can be asked to appoint one (Arbitration Act 1996).

5. The procedure for the arbitration hearing agreed by the parties can range from a 'paper' arbitration to a very formal court-like procedure.

6. The decision by the arbitrator is called an award. It is binding on the parties and can be enforced through the courts if necessary.

7. An award by an arbitrator can only be challenged in the courts on the grounds of serious irregularity in the proceedings or on a point of law (ss68, 69 Arbitration Act 1996).

8. The main advantages of arbitration are:
   - expertise – where the arbitrator has specialist knowledge;
   - flexibility – ability to choose time, place and type of procedure;
   - privacy – the facts of the dispute are not made public;
   - speed – although commercial and international arbitrations are subject to delays;
   - cost – although the use of specialist arbitrators can be expensive.

9. The main disadvantage is that legal points are not suitable for decision by a non-lawyer.

CHAPTER 7

TRIBUNALS AND ENQUIRIES

Administrative
- Created by statute
- Enforcement of social and welfare rights
- Various types –
  a) social security
  b) employment
  c) immigration etc.
- Usually panel of 3
- More informal and cheaper than court

Domestic
- Internal disciplinary
- Some created by statute, e.g. Solicitors Disciplinary Tribunal
- Some have right of appeal to Privy Council

TRIBUNALS

Control of tribunals
1 Council on Tribunals
  - created 1958
  - observes/investigates
  - makes recommendations
2 The Courts
  - judicial review
  - three prerogative orders
    a) mandamus
    b) prohibition
    c) certiorari

A system of tribunals operates alongside the court system. Each type of tribunal specialises in a certain type of case. Cases concerning these particular matters must go to the appropriate tribunal and not to a court.

7.1 ADMINISTRATIVE TRIBUNALS

1. There are over 75 different types of tribunal, with a total of more than 2000 panels around the country.
2. Almost all administrative tribunals have been created by statute. For example, the Immigration Appeals Tribunal was set up by the Immigration Act 1971, and the Mental Health Review Tribunal by the Mental Health Act 1983.
3. Note that not all have the word tribunal in their title, for example, the Criminal Injuries Compensation Appeal Panel.
4. There is an argument that tribunals are an extension of the machinery of administration rather than being purely judicial.
5. All tribunals are subject to the law of natural justice and judicial review of their proceedings.

7.1.1 Types of tribunal

1. There is considerable diversity in the jurisdiction of the various tribunals. Many tribunals are concerned with the enforcement of social and welfare rights, for example the Social Security Appeals Tribunal.
2. Some deal with compensation (e.g. Criminal Injuries Compensation Appeals Panel), others with rights to benefit (e.g. Social Security Appeals Tribunal), others with the liberty of individuals (e.g. Mental Health Review Tribunal).
3. Employment tribunals handle disputes from all aspects of work-related incidents. This includes disputed deductions from wages, unfair dismissal, redundancy and discrimination.
4. The common basis is that tribunals are forums where individuals or businesses may challenge administrative decisions affecting their rights.

7.1.2 Domestic tribunals

1. These are internal private disciplinary bodies that operate in different institutions, such as the professions, trade unions and universities.

2. Most have been set up by the particular institution, although some have been established by statute, such as the Solicitors Disciplinary Tribunal under the Solicitors Act 1974.

3. Where the tribunal was established by statute, there will usually be an appeal route from its decisions. For example, an appeal from the decision by the General Medical Council to strike off a doctor can be made to the Judicial Committee of the Privy Council.

4. All are subject to the laws of natural justice and their decisions may be judicially reviewed.

7.1.3 Composition and procedure

1. The development of tribunals has been haphazard, so there is no consistency in the type of panel used. However, the majority of tribunals have a panel of three: a legally qualified chairman and two lay members. The lay members will have some knowledge of the field in which the tribunal operates.

2. In some tribunals there may be a single adjudicator. In employment tribunals certain types of dispute may be heard by a chairman sitting alone.

3. Chairmen are appointed by the Lord Chancellor from a list of suitable applicants drawn up by the Independent Tribunal Service. This gives chairmen a degree of independence from the government and guarantees their impartiality in making decisions in cases brought against government departments.

4. There is no standard form of procedure. Hearings are more informal than in a court case, but even the degree of informality varies. For example, employment tribunals operate in a way similar to court proceedings with witnesses usually giving evidence on oath, while social security cases are dealt with in a much more informal way.

5. Tribunals generally do not have to follow precedent; again an exception is employment tribunals.

6. Most tribunals give reasons for their decision, but there are still some tribunals which do not do so.

7.1.4 Advantages and disadvantages of tribunals

1. Advantages are:
   - speed – cases are usually dealt with more quickly than in the courts;
   - cost-effectiveness – taking a case to a tribunal is much cheaper than court proceedings as there are no fees and costs are not normally awarded;
   - expertise – each tribunal operates in a specialised field and often has lay members with specialist knowledge;
   - informality – documentation is kept simple; the hearing is usually in private (employment tribunal cases are heard in public); there are no strict rules of evidence.
2. The disadvantages are:
   - some areas, e.g. social security, have very complex regulations that the applicant may not understand;
   - government funding to help an individual with a case is not available for most tribunals (except Mental Health Review Tribunals and Immigration Tribunals);
   - the individual will usually be claiming against a government department or a business, which are more likely to be represented by lawyers – this creates an imbalance between the parties;
   - failure to give reasons for a decision make it difficult to appeal.

7.2 CONTROL OF TRIBUNALS

7.2.1 Council on tribunals

1. The Franks Committee in 1957 recommended that a supervisory body should be established.
2. As a result the Council on Tribunals was set up under the Tribunals and Inquiries Act 1958 (now superseded by the Tribunals and Inquiries Act 1992).
3. The Council has 15 members who observe tribunal hearings from time to time. The Council also receives and investigates

complaints about tribunals and issues an annual report.

4. Its role is purely advisory; it can only make recommendations. For example, in 1991 it issued a set of model tribunal rules, but these rules do not have to be followed.

5. It has been called a watch dog without teeth.

7.2.2 Control by the courts

1. The main control is by judicial review. Any party to a tribunal hearing who believes that the rules of natural justice have been breached can apply to the Queen's Bench Divisional Court for the decision to be reviewed.

2. The main rules of natural justice are that:
- there is a duty to hear both sides before a decision is made (*Baldwin v Ridge* (1964));
- no one should be a judge in his own cause (*R v Altrincham Justices ex parte Pennington* (1975)).

3. Since the Human Rights Act 1998 came into effect the test for whether there is perceived bias (as opposed to actual bias) in a case is an objective one. Would the fair-minded observer consider there was a real danger of bias? (*Director General of Fair Trading v The Proprietary Association of Great Britain* (2001)).

4. The court has three 'prerogative' orders it may make when there has been a breach of natural justice. These are:
- *mandamus*, which orders the inferior court or tribunal to perform a duty, e.g. to hear a case;
- prohibition, which prevents it from hearing a case that it has no power to deal with;
- *certiorari*, which removes the decision to the High Court so that its legality can be enquired into and, if it is found to be invalid, the decision quashed.

5. For some tribunals there is an appeal route to the courts. For example, an appeal from an employment tribunal goes to the Employment Appeal Tribunal; form here there is a possible further appeal to the Court of Appeal; finally the case may be appealed to the House of Lords.

6. Where there is an appeal route, there are precedents for the tribunals below to follow and decision making should become more consistent.

7.3 INQUIRIES

1. Inquiries are set up as and when necessary to investigate a specific issue.

2. Some inquiries may be set up under a statutory power, e.g. under s49 of the Police Act 1996 the Home Secretary can do so for any matter connected to policing in an area. This power was used to set up the Macpherson Inquiry in the Stephen Lawrence case (1997–98).

3. Even if there is no statutory power, Parliament may resolve to set up an inquiry into any matter of public importance. Often a judge will be appointed to head such an inquiry, e.g. the Scott Inquiry into the sale of arms to Iraq (1996).

4. Inquiries will sit in public unless this is against the public interest. They have the power to call witnesses and order the production of relevant documents or other evidence.

5. They are a fact-finding exercise and will issue a report on the matter; they cannot make any decision on any of the issues. Their findings may, however, be used as the basis for reforming the law.

6. Inquiries are subject to judicial review. They cannot go beyond their remit as shown in *R v Chairman of Stephen Lawrence Inquiry, ex parte A* (1998), where the inquiry could not put certain questions to witnesses as its task was to examine the conduct of the police investigation into the murder of Stephen Lawrence and not to conduct a trial of the people suspected of the murder.

CHAPTER 8

POLICE POWERS

POLICE POWERS		
Power	**Statutory provision**	**Comment**
Stop and search	• s1–7 PACE • also under other Acts, e.g. Misuse of Drugs Act 1971	• only in place to which the public have access • must have reasonable grounds for suspecting stolen or prohibited goods
Search of premises	• by search warrant (s8 PACE) • to arrest someone (s17 PACE) • after arrest (ss 18 and 32 PACE) • breach of the peace	• magistrates issue warrant • warrant must be shown before search
Arrest	• with a warrant • arrestable offences (s24 PACE) • general arrest conditions (s25 PACE)	• magistrates issue warrant • warrant must be shown as soon as practicable after arrest
Detention	• ss 34–36 PACE • 24 hours normal limit • 36 hours for serious arrestable offence (96 hours with magistrates permission)	Detainee has right to: • have someone informed • have legal advice • see a copy of the Codes of Practice
Interviews	• s53 PACE • ss34–39 Criminal Justice and Public Order Act 1994 places limits on right to silence	• must be tape-recorded • those under 17 or vulnerable must have an appropriate adult present

8.1 STOP AND SEARCH

8.1.1 Powers to stop and search

1. A police constable may stop and search people and vehicles in a place to which the public has access (s1 PACE 1984).
2. A place to which the public has access includes a place where they have paid for entry; it also includes a garden or yard of a

private property where the constable has reasonable grounds for believing the person does not reside there and has not got the permission of the resident to be there.

3. In order to stop a vehicle the constable must be in uniform (s2(9)(b) PACE).

4. In order to search a person or vehicle the constable must have reasonable grounds for suspecting that he will find stolen or prohibited articles (s1(3) PACE).

5. Police officers also have specific powers to stop and search under other legislation such as the Misuse of Drugs Act 1971 and the Prevention of Terrorism (Temporary Powers) Act 1989.

8.1.2 Safeguards on the power to stop and search

1. If a constable is not in uniform then he must produce documentary evidence that he is a police officer.

2. In all cases, before commencing the search the constable must state his name and station to the suspect, specify the object of the proposed search and the grounds for proposing the search.

3. If this is not done then the search is unlawful (*Osman v DPP* (1999)).

4. If the search is in public, the constable can only request the removal of an outer coat, jacket and gloves (s2(9)(a) PACE).

5. Code of Practice A gives the police guidance on the use of the stop and search powers. In particular it points out that reasonable suspicion can never be supported on the basis on personal factors alone. Factors such as age, colour, hairstyle, manner of dress or a known previous conviction cannot be used as the sole basis on which to search.

8.2 SEARCHING PREMISES

8.2.1 Search warrants

1. A search warrant can be issued by a magistrate allowing police to search the premises named in the warrant. Such a warrant

will only be issued where there are reasonable grounds for believing that:

- a serious arrestable has been committed; and
- there is material on the premises which is likely to be of substantial value to the investigation of the offence; and
- the material is likely to be relevant evidence; and
- it is not practicable to communicate with any person entitled to grant entry to the premises or the material; or
- entry to the premises will not be granted unless a warrant is granted; or
- the purpose of the search may be frustrated or seriously prejudiced unless a constable arriving at the premises can gain immediate entry (s8 PACE).

2. A search warrant must specify the premises to be searched and, as far as possible, the articles sought.
3. A warrant only authorises one entry within one month from the date it is issued (s16(3) PACE).

8.2.2 Other powers to enter premises

1. Police may enter without a search warrant to arrest a person (on a warrant), or for an arrestable offence, or to recapture an escaped prisoner (s17 PACE).
2. If a person is arrested, the police can enter and search premises that were occupied or controlled by him (s18 PACE).
3. If a person is arrested, the police can enter and search premises in which he was at the time of arrest or immediately before the arrest. (s32 PACE)
4. There is a common law right to enter premises in order to prevent or deal with a breach of the peace. This right exists even though the breach of the peace is in private property (*McLeod v Commissioner of Police of the Metropolis* (1994)).
5. The police may enter and search any premises where the occupier consents to this.

8.2.3 Safeguards on police powers to search premises

1. Where a warrant has been issued the police are required to enter and search at a reasonable hour, unless the purpose of the search might be frustrated (s16(4) PACE and Code of Practice B para 5).
2. The police must identify themselves to the occupier of any premises searched: they must show the search warrant to him and give him a copy (s16(5) PACE). However, this need not be done on entry, but must be done before any search commences (*R v Longman* (1988)).
3. Where the entry is under ss 17 or 18, the police must give anyone present in the premises the reason for the entry. If they do not do so the entry is unlawful (*O'Loughlin v Chief Constable of Essex* (1998)).
4. The police can only exercise powers to enter and search under s32 immediately after arrest (*R v Badham* (1987)).

8.3 POWERS OF ARREST

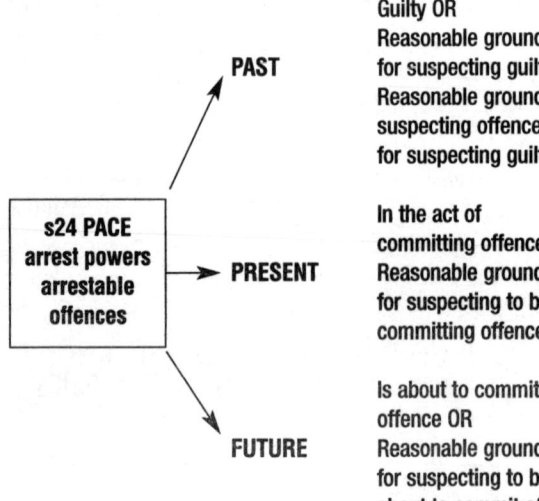

PAST — Guilty OR Reasonable grounds for suspecting guilt OR Reasonable grounds for suspecting offence AND for suspecting guilt

s24 PACE arrest powers arrestable offences

PRESENT — In the act of committing offence OR Reasonable grounds for suspecting to be committing offence

FUTURE — Is about to commit offence OR Reasonable grounds for suspecting to be about to commit offence

8.3.1 S24 Powers

1. These powers only operate where there is (or may be) an arrestable offence. An arrestable offence is:
- any offence for which the sentence is fixed by law;
- any offence for which the maximum sentence is at least five years;
- any other offence specifically made an arrestable offence.

2. Any person (police or private citizen) may arrest:
- anyone in the act of committing an arrestable offence;
- anyone whom he has reasonable grounds for suspecting to be committing such an offence;
- where an arrestable offence has been committed, anyone who is guilty of the offence or anyone whom he has reasonable grounds for suspecting to be guilty of it.

3. The police have additional powers to arrest:
- where a constable has reasonable grounds for suspecting that an arrestable offence has been committed he may arrest anyone whom he has reasonable grounds for suspecting to be guilty of the offence;
- anyone who is about to commit an arrestable offence;
- anyone whom he has reasonable grounds for suspecting to be about to commit an arrestable offence.

8.3.2 S25 powers

1. The police have power to arrest under general conditions as follows:
- the suspect's name and address cannot be discovered; or
- there are reasonable grounds for believing that the name and address given are false.

2. S25 also allows police to arrest where there are reasonable grounds for believing that arrest is necessary to prevent that person from:
- causing physical injury to himself or any other person;
- suffering physical injury;
- causing loss or damage to property;

- committing an offence against public decency;
- causing an unlawful obstruction of the highway;
- if there are reasonable grounds for believing that arrest is necessary to protect a child or other vulnerable person from the person who is arrested.

8.3.3 Arrests with a warrant

1. An application for a warrant for arrest may be made under s1 Magistrates' Court Act 1980.
2. The application must be supported by written information and also by sworn oral evidence showing that the person has committed or is suspected of committing an offence punishable by imprisonment.
3. A warrant must name the person to be arrested.

8.3.4 Other powers of arrest

1. There are some additional statutory powers to make an arrest, e.g. where a person granted police bail has failed to attend the police station on the set date (s46A PACE).
2. There is still a common law power to arrest for breach of the peace.

8.3.5 Procedure on arrest

1. It must be made clear to the person that they are being arrested and what the arrest is for.
2. Where necessary reasonable force may used to effect the arrest (s117 PACE).
3. If the arrest is made by a warrant, then that warrant must be shown on demand as soon as is reasonably practicable.
4. The police may search the arrested person for anything which might be used to make an escape or for evidence relating to the offence.
5. If the search takes place in public, the police can only require the suspect to remove outer coat, jacket and gloves.

6. If the arrest is not made at a police station, the suspect must be taken to a designated police station as soon as practicable (s30(1) PACE).
7. However, there may be a delay if it is necessary to carry out certain investigations immediately and the presence of the suspect is necessary in order to carry out those investigations (s30(10) PACE).
8. If there is a delay in taking a suspect to a police station the reasons for the delay must be recorded on arrival at the police station (s30(11) PACE).

8.4 DETENTION AT THE POLICE STATION

8.4.1 Time limits and the custody officer's role

1. For most offences a person may only be detained for a maximum of 24 hours. They must then be charged or released.
2. For serious arrestable offences detention can be authorised for another 12 hours (i.e. up to 36 hours total) by an officer of the rank of superintendent or above. An application can be made to magistrates for the period of detention to be extended further, up to a maximum of 96 hours (s44 PACE).
3. Under the Prevention of Terrorism (Temporary Provisions) Act 1989 a suspect can be detained for 48 hours and then up to another five days with permission from the Home Secretary.
4. At the beginning of the period of detention the custody officer must inform the suspect of their rights to:
   - have someone informed of the arrest (s56 PACE);
   - legal advice in private (and that advice is available free of charge) (s58 PACE);
   - consult the Codes of Practice;
   - to speak on the telephone for a reasonable time to one person (Code C).

The suspect must be given a written notice setting out these rights.

5. In the case of a serious arrestable offence, where it is believed that it will hinder investigations the right to have someone informed and the right to legal advice can be delayed for up to 36 hours.

6. Where the suspect is under 17 years old, a parent or guardian should be notified of the detention (s34(2) Children and Young Persons Act 1933).

7. The custody officer is responsible for reviewing the detention and deciding whether the person should be detained. This must be done at the outset of the detention, then after six hours, then every nine hours (s40 PACE).

8. A record of all events (such as visits to the cell by police officers, or interviews) must be made by the custody officer.

8.4.2 The right to legal advice

1. Research in the early 1990s showed that only a small percentage of people detained requested legal advice. In order to try to make legal advice more available Code of Practice C now sets out that:
   - there must be a poster in each police station advertising the right to have legal advice;
   - police officers must not dissuade a person in detention from obtaining advice;
   - the custody officer must point out the right to legal advice and if the person declines to speak to a solicitor the custody officer must record the reason for the refusal.

2. Although the right to legal advice can be delayed for a maximum of 36 hours in the case of a serious arrestable offence, the courts have held that it is only in rare cases that this right can be delayed (*R v Samuel* (1988), *R v Alladice* (1988)).

8.4.3 Interviews

1. At the start of an interview a suspect must be cautioned: 'You do not have to say anything. But it may harm your defence if you do not mention when questioned something which you later rely on in court. Anything you do say may be given in evidence.'

2. This caution emphasises that the right to silence has been eroded as the Criminal Justice and Public Order Act 1994 allows adverse inferences to be made at trial where the accused has failed in the police interview to mention facts (s34) or to account for objects, substances or marks (s36), or for his presence at a particular place (s37).

3. All interviews must be tape-recorded (s60 PACE).

4. Suspects are entitled to have a lawyer present during the interview, except where the right to legal advice has been delayed under s58 PACE in the case of a serious arrestable offence (Code of Practice C).

5. Suspects under 17 or those who are mentally disordered or handicapped must have an appropriate adult present during the interview, even if they appear to understand the questions (*R v Aspinall* (1999)).

6. There should be a short break at least every two hours, breaks for meal times, and the suspect must be allowed an eight-hour period of rest.

7. Code of Practice E sets out rules and guidelines for the conduct of interviews.

8. If a confession is obtained by oppression or in circumstances likely to render it unreliable, this evidence can be excluded by the trial judge (s76 PACE).

8.4.4 Searches, samples and fingerprinting

1. When detained at a police station, a non-intimate search may be made if the custody office believes this is necessary (s54 PACE). The search must be carried out by a person of the same sex as the suspect.

2. If a strip search involving the removal of more than outer clothing is considered necessary, then the search must:
   - take place where the suspect cannot be seen by any person who does need to be present;
   - be conducted with proper regard to the sensitivity of the person and to minimise embarrassment (Code of Practice C, Annex A).
3. An intimate search consists of the physical examination of a person's body orifices, other than the mouth.
4. An intimate search must be authorised by a superintendent or above in rank who believes that there is hidden:
   - an article which could cause harm; or
   - a Class A drug.
5. The actual search can only be carried out by a doctor or nurse, although, where it is for an article which may cause harm and a superintendent or above in rank considers it is not practicable to wait for a doctor or nurse, then a police officer may carry out the search.
6. Where the offence being investigated is a recordable offence, the police may take fingerprints (s60 PACE) and non-intimate samples, including hair (except pubic hair) and saliva (s63 PACE).
7. The consent of the person should be obtained before fingerprints or non-intimate samples are taken. If consent is refused then a police officer of the rank of superintendent or above can authorise the taking of fingerprints and non-intimate samples. Reasonable force can be used if necessary (s117 PACE).
8. Intimate samples (blood, semen or any other tissue fluid, urine, pubic hair, a dental impression or a swab taken from a body orifice other than the mouth) can only be taken by a doctor or nurse (s62 PACE).
9. Any fingerprints or samples taken must be destroyed if the person is not charged or is found not guilty. However, where a sample is not destroyed it can be used in evidence, unless the trial judge excludes it under s78 PACE (*A-G's Reference (No 3 of 1999)* (2001)).

8.5 COMPLAINTS AGAINST THE POLICE

1. Any person who believes that the police have exceeded their powers may make a complaint to the police authorities.
2. The type of complaint determines how it is dealt with. Minor complaints may be informally resolved if the complainant agrees.
3. All other complaints are investigated by the police themselves.
4. Serious complaints must be referred to the Police Complaints Authority (PCA), which was set up under PACE. The PCA will supervise the investigation. The powers of the PCA are now governed by the Police Act 1996.
5. Investigation of a serious complaint or a complaint against a senior police officer must be carried out by another police force.

8.5.1 Court actions against the police

1. Where there is an allegation that a police officer has committed a crime, e.g. assault, criminal proceedings may be taken against that police officer. These proceedings may be commenced by the Crown Prosecution Service or as a private prosecution by the victim.
2. Where there is a breach of civil rights, the individual affected may take civil proceedings and claim damages (compensation). For example, where the police have entered premises without a search warrant a claim for trespass to land may be made, or where there has been an unlawful arrest or unreasonable force a claim for trespass to the person may be made.

Crown Prosecution Service
- Prosecution of Offences Act 1985
- Take over case from police
- Can discontinue if
  a) insufficient evidence
  b) not in public interest
- Glidewell report (1998) critical; led to changes

Bail
Police bail
Bail granted by Court
- Bail Act 1976
- Presumption in favour of bail
- Can refuse if believe would fail to surrender or commit offence or interfere with witnesses

CRIMINAL PROCESS

Criminal courts
Crown Court
- indictable offences
- tried by judge and jury
Magistrates Court
- summary offences
- may send triable either way to Crown Court
- tried by a District Judge or lay magistrates

Appeals
From Magistrates to:
- Queens Bench Divisional Court by case stated
  OR
- Crown Court
From Crown Court to:
- Court of Appeal
- further appeal to House of Lords

9.1 THE CROWN PROSECUTION SERVICE (CPS)

1. The CPS was set up by the Prosecution of Offences Act 1985 as an independent prosecuting body. The head of the CPS is the Director of Public Prosecutions.

2. Once a defendant has been charged or summonsed by the police, the case file is handed over to the CPS to review.

3. The CPS may decide to discontinue a case if there is insufficient evidence or if it is not in the public interest to prosecute.
4. Section 6 of the Code for Crown Prosecutors sets out some common public interest factors considered.
5. Factors in favour of prosecution include:
   - a weapon was used;
   - the defendant was in a position of authority or trust;
   - the offence was premeditated;
   - the offence was carried out by a group;
   - the defendant has relevant previous convictions.
6. Factors against prosecution include:
   - the offence was committed as a result of a genuine mistake;
   - the loss or harm is minor and arose from a single incident;
   - the defendant is elderly or suffering from significant mental or physical illness.
7. The Glidewell Report (1998) the CPS was reorganised into 42 areas with a chief Crown Prosecutor for each area.
8. In the Magistrates' Court the CPS will be represented by a Crown Prosecutor (qualified lawyer) or by a lay prosecutor.
9. In the Crown Court, the CPS can be represented by a Crown Prosecutor who has the relevant advocacy qualification or by an independent advocate. Advocacy rights in the Crown Court were given to employed CPS lawyers by the Access to Justice Act 1999.

9.2 BAIL

Bail can be given by the police or it can be given by a court before which the defendant appears.
1. There is a presumption that bail should be granted (s4 Bail Act 1976).
2. However, bail need not be granted where there are substantial grounds for believing that the accused would, if granted bail:
   - fail to surrender to custody;
   - commit an offence while on bail;
   - interfere with witnesses or otherwise obstruct the course of justice.

3. The court can also refuse to grant bail if it is satisfied that the defendant should be kept in custody for his own protection.
4. Factors considered include:
   - the nature and seriousness of the offence;
   - the character, antecedents, associations and community ties of the defendant;
   - the defendant's record of fulfilling his obligations under previous grants of bail;
   - the strength of the evidence against the defendant.

9.2.1 Special cases

1. The presumption in favour of bail is removed where it appears that the defendant has committed a triable either way offence or an indictable offence while on bail.
2. For murder, attempted murder, manslaughter, rape or attempted rape where the defendant has already served a custodial sentence for such an offence, bail should only be granted in exceptional circumstances (s56 Crime and Disorder Act 1998).
3. The prosecution may appeal against the grant of bail where: the offence carries a maximum sentence of at least five years

9.2.2 Balancing conflicting interests

1. Individuals have a right to liberty (Human Rights Convention), but this right must be balanced against protection of the public. This balance must be considered when granting bail.
2. About 10% of those on bail commit further offences.
3. It may be possible to use a curfew as a condition of bail, with electronic tagging to monitor those at risk of committing further offences.
4. About 20% of the prison population is in custody awaiting trial. Many of these are given non-custodial sentences or a very short prison sentence which means their immediate release. These defendants are clearly not thought to be a danger to the public, but have had to stay in custody while awaiting trial.

9.3 CLASSIFICATION OF OFFENCES

Summary offences	Triable either way offences	Indictable offences
Tried in Magistrates' Court Maximum sentence 6 months and/or £5000 fine	Plea before venue ● guilty plea – magistrates decide whether to hear case ● not guilty plea – defendant's right to elect trial by jury or stay in Magistrates' Court	First administrative hearing in Magistrates' Court Case then transferred to Crown Court ● guilty plea – judge decides sentence ● not guilty plea – jury decide verdict

The trial court is determined by the category of the offence being tried. There are three categories of offence. These are:

● summary offences – the least serious and can only be tried at a Magistrates' Court;
● triable either way – the middle range of offences and can be tried in either the Magistrates' Court or the Crown Court;
● indictable – the most serious offences and can only be tried at the Crown Court.

9.4 MAGISTRATES' COURT

9.4.1 Jurisdiction of the Magistrates' Court

1. Tries all summary offences, and
2. These two categories account for about 98% of all criminal cases. 90% of defendants plead guilty. Any triable either way offence when it is decided that the offence should be tried here.
3. The maximum sentence in the Magistrates Court is six months imprisonment (6 + 6 = 12 for two offences) and a fine of £5000.
4. Conducts committal proceedings for all triable either way cases that are going to the Crown Court; the magistrates check the evidence to see if there is a *prima facie* case to go to the Crown Court.

5. Deals with the first hearing of all indictable offences; these cases are then sent to the Crown Court.
6. Decides whether to grant arrest warrants or search warrants, whether the defendant should be granted bail.
7. Youth Court hears cases involving those aged 10 to 17 inclusive in the
8. The Magistrates' Court also has civil jurisdiction. This includes:
   - licensing pubs and other venues to sell alcohol;
   - granting licences under the betting and gaming laws;
   - enforcing demands for council tax;
   - hearing family cases;
   - proceedings under the Children Act 1989.

9.4.2 Proposals for reform

1. In 1999 and 2000 the Government tried to remove the defendant's right to elect trial at the Crown Court. On both occasions the House of Lords voted against the change.
2. The Auld Review (2001) may recommend that offences punishable by up to two years imprisonment should be tried by a 'hybrid' court of a District judge and two lay magistrates.

9.4.3 The Youth Court

1. Young offenders aged 10 to 17 inclusive are tried here. The exception is young offenders charged with very serious offences including murder, manslaughter, rape, or causing death by dangerous driving, who must be tried at the Crown Court. In addition, other serious offences (carrying a sentence of 14 years imprisonment or more for an adult) may be tried in the Crown Court.
2. There must be three magistrates on the bench with a mix of sexes, and the magistrates in the Youth Court have special training.
3. The procedure is less formal than in the adult court, with only authorised persons present.

4. A parent or guardian must be present where the offender is under 16, unless it would be unreasonable to require such attendance in the circumstances.

9.5 APPEALS FROM THE MAGISTRATES' COURT

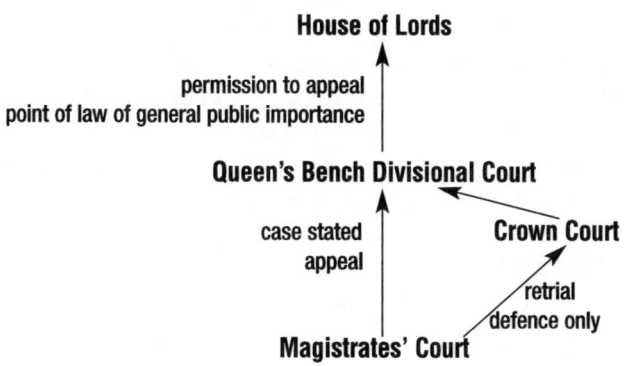

There are two different appeal routes.

1. Case stated appeal to the Queen's Bench Divisional Court.
   a) This is used where the appeal is on a point of law – the magistrates are asked to state a case (finding of facts). The (QBCO) can quash the decision, confirm it or remit the case to the Magistrates' Court for a re-hearing.
   b) This route is available for both prosecution and defence.
   c) A further appeal is possible to the House of Lords. This must be on a point of law of general public importance and the House of Lords (or QBD) must give permission to appeal. This is only used a few times each year.

2. The Crown Court.
   a) This route is only available to the defendant. The appeal can be on sentence or conviction or both.
   b) The whole case is reheard at the Crown Court by a judge and two lay magistrates.
   c) There is no further appeal, unless a point of law is involved when the appeals then goes to the QBD as above.

9.6 THE CROWN COURT

1. The Crown Court sits in about 90 centres.

2. Once a case has been transferred from the Magistrates' Court, a plea and directions hearing will be held to establish whether the plea is guilty or not guilty and to identify key issues for the trial.

3. If the defendant pleads guilty the judge will decide the sentence.

4. If the defendant pleads not guilty, the trial is held before a judge and a jury of twelve. The judge decides the law and the jury decides the facts. The jury decides whether the defendant is guilty or not guilty. This can be by a unanimous verdict or by a majority verdict (11 to 1 or 10 to 2).

9.7 APPEALS FROM THE CROWN COURT

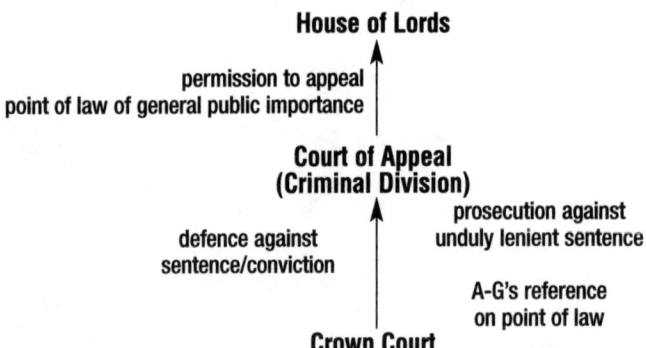

House of Lords

permission to appeal
point of law of general public importance

Court of Appeal (Criminal Division)

defence against sentence/conviction

prosecution against unduly lenient sentence

A-G's reference on point of law

Crown Court

The defendant may appeal against conviction and or sentence. The prosecution has very limited rights of appeal, although these may be increased in the future. The Law Commission has recommended that the prosecution should have a right to appeal against a judge's ruling on a point of law. It has also recommended that the prosecution should have the right to appeal against an acquittal in the case of murder where there is compelling new evidence.

9.7.1 Appeals by the defendant

1. The defendant may appeal against conviction and/or sentence to the Court of Appeal (Criminal Division). In all cases the defendant needs leave to appeal from the Court of Appeal, or the trial judge must grant a certificate that the case is fit for appeal.
2. The only ground for allowing an appeal against conviction is that the conviction is unsafe (s2(1) Criminal Appeal Act 1968 as amended by the Criminal Appeal Act 1995).
3. If the Court of Appeal allows the defendant's appeal, it may order a retrial (s7 Criminal Appeal Act 1968 as amended by the Criminal Justice Act 1988) or it may quash the conviction.
4. When hearing an appeal, the Court of Appeal has power to admit fresh evidence if it is necessary or expedient in the interests of justice (s23(1) Criminal Appeal Act 1968).

9.7 2 Appeals by the prosecution

1. The prosecution may apply to the High Court for an order to quash an acquittal because of interference with a witness or the jury (s54 Criminal Procedure and Investigations Act 1996).
2. Following an acquittal the Attorney-General may refer a point of law to the Court of Appeal (Criminal Division). This does not affect the acquittal; it merely states the law for future cases (s36 Criminal Justice Act 1972).
3. The Attorney-General may (with leave from the Court of Appeal) refer an unduly lenient sentence to the Court of Appeal for them to review the sentence. (s36 Criminal Justice Act 1988) The Court of Appeal can quash the original sentence and impose a more severe sentence.

9.7.3 Appeals to the House of Lords

1. Both the prosecution and the defence have the right to appeal from the Court of Appeal (Criminal Division) to the House of Lords.

2. In any case the Court of Appeal must have certified that the case involves a point of law of general public importance, and either the Court of Appeal or the House of Lords must give leave to appeal (s33(2) Criminal Appeal Act 1968).

3. There is no appeal to the House of Lords on sentence.

9.8 MISCARRIAGES OF JUSTICE

9.8.1 The Criminal Case Review Commission

1. The Criminal Case Review Commission (CCRC) was set up in 1997 under the Criminal Appeal Act 1995.

2. Prior to this the responsibility for referring possible miscarriages of justice back to the Court of Appeal lay with the Home Secretary. This was criticised as being too involved with the executive and an ineffective method of dealing with possible miscarriages of justice.

3. The CCRC can investigate cases which were tried in the Crown Court or the Magistrates' Court. Where the case was tried in the Crown Court it may be referred to the Court of Appeal; where the trial was in the Magistrates' Court, the referral is to the Crown Court.

4. The CCRC can only refer a case if:
- an appeal has been decided or leave to appeal has been refused; and
- it considers there is a real possibility that the conviction (or sentence) would not be upheld (s13 Criminal Appeal Act 1995).

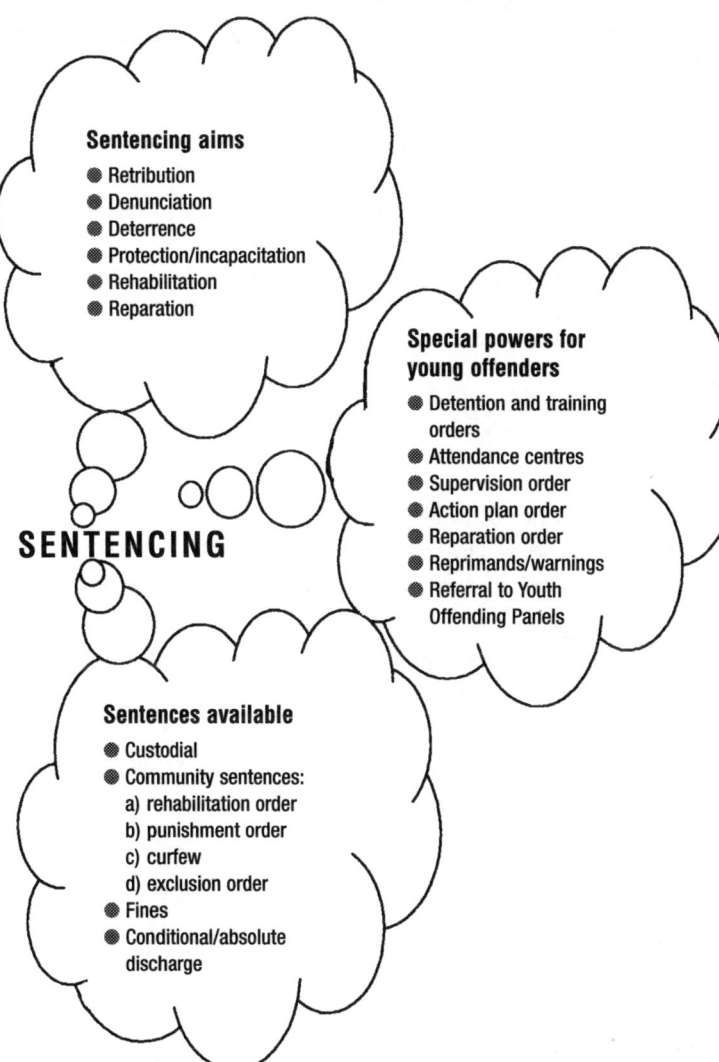

Sentencing aims
- Retribution
- Denunciation
- Deterrence
- Protection/incapacitation
- Rehabilitation
- Reparation

Special powers for young offenders
- Detention and training orders
- Attendance centres
- Supervision order
- Action plan order
- Reparation order
- Reprimands/warnings
- Referral to Youth Offending Panels

SENTENCING

Sentences available
- Custodial
- Community sentences:
  a) rehabilitation order
  b) punishment order
  c) curfew
  d) exclusion order
- Fines
- Conditional/absolute discharge

1. A distinguishing feature of the criminal law is that there is the possibility of the State imposing a punishment on an offender. Hart's definition of punishment is that it must:
   - involve pain or other unpleasant consequences;
   - be for an offence against legal rules;
   - be intentionally administered by human beings other than the offender;
   - be imposed and administered by an authority constituted by a legal system against which the offence is committed.
2. Before punishment is imposed, the sentencer should consider which aim(s) of sentencing to use, background factors (reports, etc.) and the sentences available.
3. The courts' power to sentence is contained in the Power of Criminal Courts (Sentencing) Act 2000 (PCC(S)A), which consolidates previous sentencing enactments.

10.1 AIMS OF SENTENCING

1. These are concerned with the purpose or objective that the sentencer or policy maker is seeking to achieve.
2. There are different sentencing aims that recognise the different needs of the offender, the victim and society. These needs may be in conflict.
3. Changes in penal policies can lead to one or more sentencing aims being preferred over others.
4. The main sentencing aims are retribution, denunciation, deterrence, protection of society, rehabilitation and reparation.

10.1.1 Retribution

1. This is punishment for wrong doing. It is thought of as being 'an eye for an eye' and 'a tooth for a tooth', and society's revenge for the offence.
2. Its literal form is in the death penalty for murder: a life for a life. A literal interpretation is not practical for most offences and the aim is to 'let the punishment fit the crime'.

3. Retribution is based on blameworthiness, so a mentally ill offender should not be subjected to retribution.

4. Retribution is also based on proportionality or 'just deserts', so that the sentence reflects the seriousness of the offence. This concept is supported by the use of tariff sentences and Court of Appeal guidelines.

5. Retribution can be seen in our sentencing legislation where one of the reasons for a court to pass a custodial sentence is that the offence was so serious that only a custodial sentence can be justified for the offence. Originally s1 Criminal Justice Act 1991 and is now contained in s79(2)(a) of the Powers of Criminal Courts (Sentencing) Act 2000 (PCC(S)A).

10.1.2 Denunciation

1. This is expressing society's outrage at the offence committed.

2. It emphasises the criminality of the offence, but it goes beyond retribution in that society's expectations are also considered.

3. Denunciation is the main aim behind long prison sentences being imposed for offences of causing death by dangerous driving.

4. Failure by the courts to punish in accordance with society's expectations may lead to people taking action themselves, e.g. vigilantes.

10.1.3 Deterrence

1. There are two forms of deterrence:
   - individual deterrence;
   - general deterrence.

2. Individual deterrence is aimed at the particular offender. It aims to make the experience of punishment so unpleasant that the individual will not re-offend. Alternatively a threat (such as a suspended sentence) is used to deter.

3. General deterrence is aimed at discouraging others from committing that type of offence.

4. Deterrence is based on the assumption that potential offenders will consider the consequences of their actions.

In fact, most offences are committed on the spur of the moment, so any deterrent effect is minimal.

5. Deterrence is not concerned with fairness or proportionality; the sentence imposed, especially for general deterrence, is likely to be harsher than the normal tariff for the offence.

10.1.4 Protection of society

1. This is usually achieved by incapacitation of the offender so that he or she cannot commit further offences. The ultimate example is the death penalty.

2. The sentence used to achieve incapacitation may be more severe than that needed for retribution. This conflict has been called 'deservedness versus dangerousness' (von Hirsch).

3. In our penal system a long custodial sentence is the usual method of incapacitation. This is encouraged by our sentencing legislation, as a custodial sentence should be used where the offence is a violent or sexual offence and only a custodial sentence would be adequate to protect the public from serious harm by the offender (s79(2)(b) PCC(S)A).

4. Incapacitation is also a main aim in the use of mandatory life imprisonment for a second serious sexual or violent crime (s109 PCC(S)A).

5. There are other sentences which rely on incapacitation. For example, disqualification from driving; or disqualification from owning an animal for an offence of cruelty.

6. Electronic tagging gives a degree of incapacitation while allowing the offender to remain in the community.

10.1.5 Rehabilitation

1. This aims to reform the offender and so reduce the likelihood of future re-offending.

2. A sentence aimed at rehabilitation is considered an individualised sentence as opposed to the tariff sentences given under the retributive aim. Individualised sentences can lead to apparent inconsistency in sentencing.

3. It is now accepted that imprisonment has only limited rehabilitative effect.

4. A range of other penalties have been developed aimed at rehabilitation. These include community rehabilitation orders, drug treatment and testing orders and, for young offenders, action plan orders.

5. Re-offending rates, however, show that those given community rehabilitation orders are almost as likely to re-offend as those given custodial sentences.

6. Rehabilitation is particularly important for young offenders to try to break the cycle of re-offending.

10.1.6 Reparation or restitution

1. There has been increasing concern that victims are not adequately considered when sentencing the offender.

2. Compensation orders are used instead of or in addition to the sentence imposed on the offender as reparation to the victim.

3. If the court does not make a compensation order when it has power to do so, then it must give reasons for not doing so (s130 PCC(S)A).

4. Community punishment orders involve the offender doing a certain number of hours work on community projects. This has an element of reparation to society at large.

5. A reparation order can be made where the offender is under 18. This can order reparation to the victim or the community at large (s73 PCC(S)A).

10.2 TYPES OF SENTENCE

10.2.1 Custodial sentences

1. Murder carries a mandatory sentence of life imprisonment for offenders aged 18 and over. Offenders under 18 who are convicted of murder are detained at Her Majesty's pleasure (s90 PCC(S)A).

2. For other offences a prison sentence up to the maximum for the particular offence can be imposed on offenders aged 18 and over. Offenders under 18 who are convicted of serious offences may be detained for a set period up to the maximum for the offence.

3. Offenders aged 18–20 may serve their sentence in a prison or Young Offenders Institution (s61 Criminal Justice and Court Services Act 2000).

4. Offenders aged 12–17 can be sentenced to a detention and training order for a specified period of between four and 24 months. For those under 15 years old such an order can only be made if the offender is a persistent offender (s100 PCC(S)A).

10.2.2 Minimum sentences

1. There is a mandatory life sentence where the offender has committed a second serious sexual or violent offence (s109 PCC(S)A).

2. Offenders convicted of a third offence of class A drug trafficking must be sentenced to a minimum of seven years imprisonment (s110 PCC(S)A).

3. Offenders convicted of a third offence of burglary must be sentenced to a minimum of three years imprisonment (s111 PCC(S)A).

10.2.3 Community sentences

The Government emphasis has been on extending the types of community sentences available and on making them 'tougher' so that they are not seen as a soft option. The first four in the list are for those aged 16 or over.

1. A community rehabilitation order (formerly a probation order) places the offender under supervision of a probation officer (s41 PCC(S)A).

2. A community punishment order (formerly a community service order) requires the offender to do unpaid work of 40 to 240 hours on a community project (S46 PCC(S)A).

3. The two orders above may be combined as a community punishment and rehabilitation order (s51 PCC(S)A).

4. A drug treatment and testing order can be ordered where the defendant is dependent on, or has a propensity to misuse drugs (s52 PCC(S)A).

5. A drug abstinence order can be made on an offender age 18 or over for a period of between six months and three years (s58A PCC(S)A).

6. An exclusion order prohibits the offender from entering a specified place or places. (s40A PCC(S)A). The order may last for up to two years for offenders over 16, or three months for offenders under 16.

7. A curfew order requires the offender to be present at a specified place for between two and 12 hours a day (s37 PCC(S)A). The order can last for up to six months for offenders aged 16 and over, or three months for offenders under 16. The offender's whereabouts will be monitored. This may be done by electronic tagging.

8. An attendance centre order can be imposed on offenders under 21. Attendance is for a maximum of 36 hours for offenders aged 16 to 20 and 24 hours for offenders under 16 (s60 PCC(S)A).

10.3 OTHER POWERS OF THE COURT

1. A fine can be imposed for any offence. There is no limit to the amount which the Crown Court can fine an offender. The maximum fine in the Magistrates' Court is £5000, except for health and safety offences where it is £20,000.

2. There are limits on the amount young offenders can be fined:
   - 10–13 year olds maximum £250;
   - 14–17 year olds maximum £1000.

3. A conditional discharge may be given for a period of up to three years on the condition that during this time the offender does not re-offend (s12 PCC(S)A).

4. An absolute discharge may be given. This has no conditions attached; the matter is at an end.

5. Disqualification from driving can be ordered for driving offences and also for non-driving offences, e.g. theft (s146 PCC(S)A).

10.4 ADDITIONAL POWERS IN RESPECT OF YOUNG OFFENDERS (10–17)

1. A supervision order may be made placing the offender under the supervision of a local authority or a probation officer or a member of a youth offending team for up to three years (s63 PCC(S)A).

2. An action plan order is a three-month intensive programme under which the offender may be required to do a number of things, e.g. participate in set activities, make reparation or stay away from certain places (s69 PCC(S)A).

3. A reparation order for a maximum of 24 hours work can be made (s73 PCC(S)A). The reparation may be direct to the victim if the victim agrees, or it can be to the community at large.

4. A reprimand or a warning may be given. These are not sentences imposed by a court. They are methods by which the police may deal with a young offender without taking the case to court.

5. Referral to a youth offender team must be ordered where an offender who has no previous convictions has pleaded guilty to an offence in court. Referral is also obligatory after a warning.

6. An offender's parent or guardian may be bound over for a period of up to three years to take proper care and exercise proper control of the offender (s150 PCC(S)A).

7. A parenting order requiring parents to attend counselling or guidance sessions can be made when an offender under the age of 18 is convicted of an offence. The order is also available in civil proceedings where the court makes a child safety order or an anti-social behaviour order (s8 Crime and Disorder Act 1998).

10.5 Mentally ill offenders

1. In addition to the normal range of penalties there are special powers available to the court to deal with an offender who is mentally ill.
2. The main powers are:
   - to add a condition to a probation order that the offender attends for treatment; or
   - make a hospital order to enable the offender to receive appropriate treatment as an in-patient; or
   - where the offender is a danger to the community, make a restriction order sending the offender to a secure hospital (s41 Mental Health Act 1983).

10.6 Other factors in sentencing

10.6.1 Factors surrounding the offence

1. The level of seriousness of the offence within its type is important, e.g. the amount stolen, the seriousness of injuries inflicted, the type of weapon used.
2. Other factors that aggravate an offence include:
   - premeditation;
   - a vulnerable victim;
   - an abuse of trust;
   - being the ring leader.
3. Where the offender has pleaded not guilty, these facts will have been given as part of the evidence.
4. Where the offender has pleaded guilty, the facts of the case are outlined to the court by the prosecution. If the defendant does not agree with prosecution version, then a Newton hearing is held to establish the facts.

10.6.2 The offender's background

1. Previous convictions of the offender or any failure to respond to previous sentences may be taken into account in considering the seriousness of the offence (s151 PCC(S)A).
2. The stage in the court proceedings at which the defendant pleaded guilty to the offence is considered. An early guilty plea is likely to result in a less severe sentence than would otherwise have been imposed (s152 PCC(S)A). However, credit need not be given in exceptional cases (*Scarley* (2001)).
3. Pre-sentence reports on the offender and his background may be available for the court.

CHAPTER 11

THE LEGAL PROFESSION

LEGAL PROFESSION

SOLICITORS	BARRISTERS
Training	**Training**

Degree, if not in law then must do
Common Professional Examination

● Legal Practice Course	● Bar Vocational Course
● Training contract	● Pupillage

Role	**Role**
● Private practice in solicitors' firm	● Self-employed in chambers
● Wide variety of work	● Mostly court work
● Contracts, leases, wills conveyancing etc.	● Also write opinions and draft documents
● Direct access by clients	● Direct access limited to other professions, e.g. accountants

May be employed in CPS, CDS, local
authority, etc. or private commercial business

Advocacy rights	**Advocacy rights**
Advocacy certificate (Courts and Legal Services Act 1990) Full rights (Access to Justice Act 1999)	Full rights

Supervision	**Supervision**
Law Society	Bar Council

Legal Services Ombudsman

11.1 SOLICITORS

11.1.1 Training

1. To become a solicitor it is usual to have a law degree. If a
   student has a degree in another subject it is necessary to take
   the Common Professional Examination (CPE).

2. The next stage is the one-year Legal Practice Course (LPC), which includes training in skills such as client interviewing, negotiation and advocacy.

3. After passing this the student must then obtain a training contract. This can be with a firm of solicitors, or in an organisation such as the Crown Prosecution Service (CPS) or the legal department of a local authority. The training contract is for a period of two years and gives the trainee solicitor practical experience.

4. A 20-day Professional Skills Course must be completed during the training period.

5. After completing all the above the trainee will be admitted as a solicitor by the Law Society.

6. There is also a route for non-graduate mature students to qualify. This is by becoming a fellow of the Institute of Legal Executives (must be over 25 years, have passed Part I and Part II ILEX examinations and have worked in a solicitor's office for at least five years). They must then take the LPC examinations.

11.1.2 Role

1. The majority of those who qualify as solicitors will work in private practice in a solicitor's firm.

2. Initially they will work as an assistant solicitor in a firm, but may eventually become a partner or set up on their own as a sole practitioner.

3. There is no maximum on the number of partners in a firm of solicitors. The size of firms varies from the sole practitioner to partnerships with over 100 partners and several hundred assistant solicitors.

4. The work of a solicitor will vary according to the type of firm. Small high street firms are likely to concentrate on family law, wills and probate, housing law, consumer law and criminal law. Large city firms specialise in business and commercial law.

5. Other careers are available as an employed lawyer in an organisation such as the CPS, Civil Service or Local

Authority. Solicitors are also employed by private businesses as legal advisors.

11.1.3 Advocacy rights

1. Solicitors in private practice can also act as advocates. They have always had full advocacy rights in the Magistrates' Court and the County Court.
2. The Courts and Legal Services Act 1990 allowed them to apply for an advocacy certificate for rights in the higher courts, but only about 1% applied for a certificate.
3. The Access to Justice Act 1999 provides that all solicitors will be given full rights of audience. The Law Society is to bring in new training requirements to ensure that newly qualified solicitors will automatically have advocacy rights.
4. Solicitors employed by the CPS may act as a prosecutor-advocate in any court for which they hold an advocacy qualification.
5. Solicitors employed by the Legal Services Commission may act as an advocate to represent members of the public in any court for which they hold an advocacy qualification.
6. Other employed solicitors only have rights of audience to represent their employer.

11.2 BARRISTERS

11.2.1 Training

1. To qualify as a barrister it is usual to have a law degree. If a student has a degree in another subject then it is necessary to take the Common Professional Examination (CPE).
2. Would-be barristers must then take the Bar Vocational Course (BVC), which places emphasis on practical skills of drafting pleadings and advocacy.
3. All students must also become a member of one of the four Inns of Court and must either dine at that Inn a set number of times or attend weekend courses run by the Inn.

4. After passing the BVC and completing the necessary attendance at an Inn of Court, the person is called to the Bar and is officially qualified as a barrister. However, before they can appear in court they must do a 12-month period of pupillage, 'work-shadowing' a barrister.

11.2.2 Role

1. Barristers at the Bar are self-employed. They usually practise from chambers, sharing expenses of rent, secretarial staff, etc.

2. They are independent and can be briefed by any solicitor. In addition, some professions, such as accountants and surveyors, can deal directly with a barrister.

3. A member of the public can only brief a barrister via a solicitor, though there is pressure for direct access to barristers to be allowed.

4. The majority of barristers concentrate on advocacy and they have rights of audience in all courts. Their other work involves giving advice and opinions on points of law or potential cases and drafting papers for court.

5. Some barristers specialising in areas such as taxation or patent law will rarely appear in court.

6. Employed barristers can work for the CPS, Government departments, local authorities or businesses. Employed barristers now retain their rights of audience though there are limits on who they may represent (Access to Justice Act 1999).

7. After being qualified for ten years a barrister may apply to 'take silk' and become a Queen's Counsel (QC). QCs are appointed by the Lord Chancellor.

11.3 PARA-LEGALS

11.3.1 Legal executives

1. To become a Fellow of the Institute of Legal Executives (ILEX) it is necessary to be over 25 years of age, to have passed the ILEX Part I and Part II examinations and to have worked in a solicitor's firm (or other comparable employment, e.g. CPS) for at least five years.

2. Legal executives work in solicitors' firms and deal with the more straightforward cases.

3. They have limited rights of audience in the County Court to make unopposed applications.

11.3.2 Licensed conveyancers

1. These specialise in the conveyancing of property.

2. Complaints about licensed conveyancers are dealt with by the Legal Services Ombudsman.

11.4 REGULATION OF THE LEGAL PROFESSIONS

11.4.1 The Law Society

1. This is the governing body of solicitors.

2. It is a regulatory body that can set rules and discipline solicitors.

3. It also acts as the representative of the interests of solicitors.

4. The Office for the Supervision of Solicitors was set up in 1996 to investigate complaints by clients against individual solicitors. As it is funded by the Law Society it is criticised for not being independent. There have also been problems with delays in handling complaints.

5. Serious complaints against solicitors are heard by the Solicitors Disciplinary Council. This Council has the power to strike off solicitors.

11.4.2 The Bar Council

1. This is the governing body of barristers.

2. As with the Law Society, it has both regulatory and representative functions.

3. Complaints by clients about barristers can be investigated by the Lay Complaints Commissioner, who has the power to order a compensation payment for poor service.
4. The Senate of the Inns of Court will hear serious complaints and has the power to disbar a barrister.

11.4.3 The Legal Services Ombudsman

1. The post of Legal Services Ombudsman was set up by the Courts and Legal Services Act 1990.
2. The Ombudsman oversees solicitors, barristers and licensed conveyancers.
3. The Ombudsman investigates whether complaints have been properly handled by the regulatory bodies.
4. The Access to Justice Act 1999 gave the Ombudsman power to order payment of compensation by an individual lawyer or firm.

11.4.4 Suing a lawyer

1. There is a contract between a solicitor and client. So, if there is a breach of contract, the client has the right to sue the solicitor. There is no contract between a client and their barrister.
2. It is possible for a client to sue both solicitors and barristers for negligence. In some cases where the negligence has caused loss to a third person, that person may be able to sue (*White v Jones* (1995)).
3. It used not to be possible to sue either a barrister or a solicitor for negligent advocacy (*Rondel v Worsley* (1969), *Saif Ali v Sydney Mitchell and Co.* (1980)). However, this rule was changed in the case of *Hall v Simons* (2000) and it is now possible to sue for negligent advocacy.

11.5 THE FUTURE OF THE LEGAL PROFESSIONS

1. There is criticism that the Law Society and the Bar Council have been too slow to change their own rules to allow reforms in the Courts and Legal Services Act 1990 (CLSA) and the Access to Justice Act 1999 (AJA) to take effect.

2. An example of this is that multi-disciplinary practices allowed by s66 CLSA are still barred by the regulations of the two governing bodies.

3. The Access to Justice Act 1999 has set the foundations for solicitors and barristers to have the same rights of litigation and advocacy. This can be seen as a move towards fusion, as there will be no difference in the work that can be undertaken by the two branches of the profession.

4. The Legal Services Consultative Panel, set up by the Access to Justice Act 1999, has been asked by the Lord Chancellor to monitor and advise on whether the professions should retain their right to be self-regulating.

5. In March 2000 the Office of Fair Trading issued a report on unjustified restrictions on competition which were thought to limit consumer choice. The main points made by this report were:

   - restrictions on direct access to barristers require customers to employ two types of lawyer where one might do;
   - the rules preventing the establishment of multi-disciplinary practices should be relaxed to bring together accountants, lawyers and other professionals such as surveyors and estate agents;
   - the restriction preventing barristers from forming partnerships with each other was questioned;
   - the distinction between QCs and junior barristers was believed to have significant effects on competition, and the value of the present system of QCs to consumers was questioned.

CHAPTER 12

THE JUDICIARY

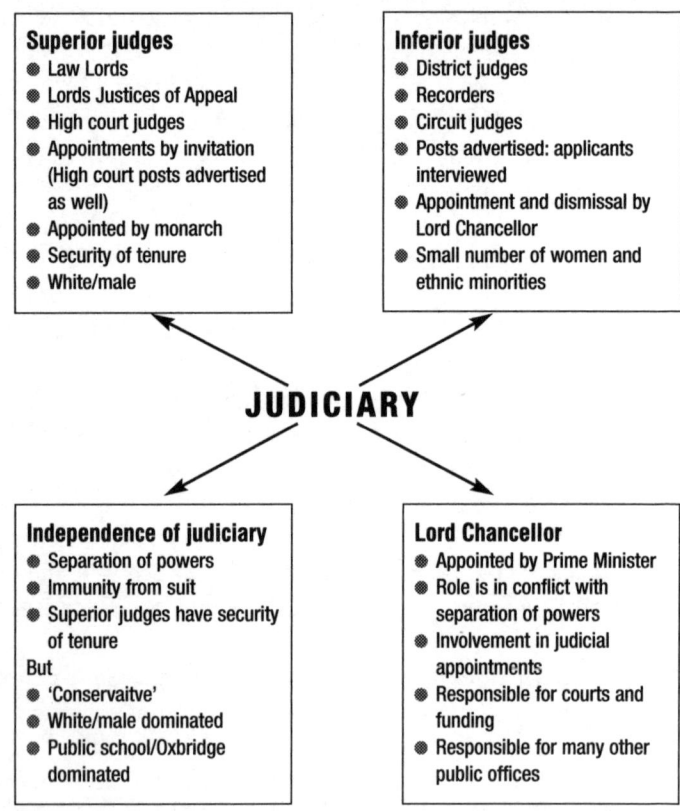

Superior judges
- Law Lords
- Lords Justices of Appeal
- High court judges
- Appointments by invitation (High court posts advertised as well)
- Appointed by monarch
- Security of tenure
- White/male

Inferior judges
- District judges
- Recorders
- Circuit judges
- Posts advertised: applicants interviewed
- Appointment and dismissal by Lord Chancellor
- Small number of women and ethnic minorities

JUDICIARY

Independence of judiciary
- Separation of powers
- Immunity from suit
- Superior judges have security of tenure

But
- 'Conservaitve'
- White/male dominated
- Public school/Oxbridge dominated

Lord Chancellor
- Appointed by Prime Minister
- Role is in conflict with separation of powers
- Involvement in judicial appointments
- Responsible for courts and funding
- Responsible for many other public offices

Judges can be divided into two main types: inferior judges and superior judges. These categories affect the way judges are appointed, the courts they sit in and the way they can be dismissed.

12.1 APPOINTMENT

1. The professional qualifications needed to become a judge are set out in the Courts and Legal Services Act 1990. They are based on advocacy rights at the appropriate level of court.

2. The policy of the Lord Chancellor on applications for judicial posts states that appointments are made on merit, and the skills needed (such as intellectual and analytical ability) are set out in Annual Report on Judicial Appointments.

3. Judicial posts up to the level of circuit judge are advertised. High Court posts are also advertised but the Lord Chancellor reserves the right to invite someone who has not applied.

4. For inferior judges a formal interview is used as part of the appointment system.

5. For High Court judges confidential 'soundings' of senior judges are used as part of the decision-making process.

12.1.1 Inferior judges

1. District Judges sit in the County Court and Magistrates' Court. They:
   - must have had a general qualification (i.e. be a barrister or a solicitor) for at least seven years;
   - will usually be appointed a Deputy District Judge for two years first;
   - are appointed by the Lord Chancellor.

2. Recorders are part-time judges who can sit in the County Court and the Crown Court. They:
   - must have a ten-year County Court or Crown Court qualification;
   - are appointed for a renewable period of five years;
   - must sit for at least 15–30 days per year;
   - are appointed by the Queen on the recommendation of the Lord Chancellor.

   The five-year term of office and the abolition of the post of Assistant Recorder were announced in 2000. This was to try to ensure that judges would be considered sufficiently independent of the executive for the purposes of the European Convention on Human Rights (*Starrs v Procurator Fiscal* (1999)).

3. Circuit judges are full-time judges who sit in the County Court and/or Crown Court. They:

- must have a ten-year County Court or Crown Court qualification, or be a recorder, or have held another judicial post (e.g. District Judge) for at least three years;
- are appointed by the Queen on the recommendation of the Lord Chancellor.

12.1.2 Superior judges

1. High Court judges or puisne judges sit in the High Court. They will be appointed to one of the three divisions (Queen's Bench, Chancery or Family). They:
   - must have a ten-year High Court qualification or have been a Circuit Judge for at least two years;
   - are appointed by the Queen on the recommendation of the Lord Chancellor;
   - will usually have sat as a Deputy High Court judge before being appointed.
2. Lords Justices of Appeal sit in the Court of Appeal. They:
   - must have a ten-year High Court qualification or be a High Court judge (this is the normal route);
   - are appointed by the Queen on the advice of the Prime Minister.
3. Lords of Appeal in Ordinary sit in the House of Lords and are also known as the Law Lords. They:
   - must have held high judicial office for two years or have held a Supreme Court Qualification for 15 years;
   - are appointed by the Queen on the advice of the Prime Minister.

12.1.3 Criticism of the appointment system

1. The Lord Chancellor has too much influence in appointments.
2. There is an emphasis on the 'old boy' network, with the use of secret soundings.
3. The old boy network shows in the fact that the majority of new appointments for High Court judges come from sets of barristers where ex-members are judges.

4. There have been only two solicitors appointed to the High Court bench; one in 1993 after serving as a Circuit judge; the second in 2000 direct from practising as a solicitor.
5. There are only a small number of women judges, especially in the High Court and above. There has never been a female judge in the House of Lords.
6. The number of judges from ethnic minorities is very small – less than 1% of Circuit judges and none in the High Court or above.
7. The majority of judges in the High Court and above have been to public school and Oxbridge. *Labour Research* magazine found that of new appointments in 1997–99, 73% had been to public school and 79% to Oxbridge.
8. A Judicial Appointments Commissioner was appointed in 2001, but his role is only to keep the appointment process under review. He does not advise on actual appointments.

12.2 TRAINING

1. This is organised by the Judicial Studies Board (JSB).
2. For most new judges there is a short residential course (three or four days).
3. New Recorders also have to visit two penal establishments and sit in on trials at a Crown Court.
4. Most judges will attend a continuation seminar once every three years.
5. There are additional special training schemes for new areas of law such as the introduction of the Human Rights Act 1998.
6. Part-time judges are subject to appraisal schemes.
7. There is criticism that the training of judges is inadequate, in particular that the initial course for Recorders is too short, as lawyers who are not criminal law practitioners will be expected to sit on criminal cases.

12.3 REMOVAL

1. It is seen as important that judges should be independent, so they must be protected from removal at the whim of the Government.
2. As a result, superior judges have security of tenure that dates back to the Act of Settlement 1701. They can only be removed by the Queen following a petition presented to her by both Houses of Parliament.
3. The Lord Chancellor can, however, declare vacant the office of any judge who, through ill-health, is incapable of carrying out his work and of taking the decision to resign.
4. Inferior judges can be dismissed by the Lord Chancellor for incapacity or misbehaviour (s17(4) Courts Act 1971).
5. In 2000, the Lord Chancellor set out that persistent failure to comply with sitting requirements, failure to comply with training requirements, or sustained failure to observe the standards reasonably expected would be grounds for removal from office.
6. The Lord Chancellor also laid down that a nominated judge would carry out an investigation and that the Lord Chief Justice would have to concur with any decision taken by the Lord Chancellor to remove a judge.
7. In reality, a judge will normally resign rather than wait to be removed from office.

12.4 INDEPENDENCE OF THE JUDICIARY

12.4.1 Doctrine of the separation of powers

1. This doctrine was first put forward by Montesquieu in the eighteenth century.
2. The theory is that the three primary functions of the State (legislature, executive and judicial) must be kept separate in order to safeguard the rights citizens.

3. In our Government the legislature is Parliament, the executive is the Cabinet and the judiciary is the judges.
4. There is an overlap of the legislature and executive as the Cabinet are also members of Parliament.
5. The Lord Chancellor's role goes across all three arms of State.

12.4.2 The judiciary

1. The Lord Chancellor is appointed by the Prime Minister and holds office only while the Prime Minister wishes.
2. The fact that the Lord Chancellor plays a major role in appointing or recommending judicial appointments does compromise the independence of judges.
3. The fact that the Prime Minister recommends the most senior judges (Heads of Division, Lords Justices of Appeal and Law Lords) for appointment could also compromise the independence of the judiciary.

12.4.3 Protection of judicial independence

1. Judges have immunity from being sued for anything they do in the course of their judicial duties (*Sirros v Moore* (1975)).
2. By convention, individual judges are not criticised during Parliamentary debates.
3. Judicial salaries are paid from the consolidated fund so that payment is made without the need for Parliamentary authorisation.
4. The security of tenure of superior judges protects them from the threat of removal.

12.4.4 Bias

1. Judges are viewed as too pro-establishment and conservative with a small 'c'. Professor Griffiths cites cases such as *Attorney-General v Guardian Newspapers Ltd* (1987) and *R v Secretary of State for the Home Office, ex parte Brind* (1991) to support this view.

2. Natural justice demands that no man be a judge in his own cause. In addition, a judge who is involved, whether personally or as a director of a company, in promoting the same causes as one of the parties to the action, is automatically disqualified from hearing the case (*In Re Pinochet Ugarte* (1999)).

3. The test for bias on the material circumstances of a judge's involvement is an objective test, i.e. whether or not the fair-minded observer would consider that there was a real danger of bias (*Director General of Fair Trading v The Proprietary Association of Great Britain* (2001)).

12.5 THE LORD CHANCELLOR'S ROLE

1. The Lord Chancellor is appointed by the Prime Minister and can be dismissed by him at any time. The Lord Chancellor will change with a change of Government.

2. The Lord Chancellor is involved in all three arms of State. He is:
   - the speaker of the House of Lords when it is sitting in its legislative capacity;
   - a member of the Cabinet (the executive);
   - head of the judiciary and can sit as a judge in the House of Lords and the Privy Council.

3. The Lord Chancellor plays a major role in the appointment of judges.

4. The Lord Chancellor's Department has responsibility for the courts, tribunals and the Community Legal Service.

5. The Department also oversees the work of a number of other offices including the Official Solicitor's Department, the Land Registry and the Public Trustee Office.

CHAPTER 13

LAY PEOPLE IN THE LEGAL SYSTEM

Lay magistrates	Juries
● 21 to 65 on appointment ● Unlikely to be under 27 ● Can sit to age 70	● 18–70 ● Over 65s have right to be excused
● Live within 15 miles of Commission area ● Possess six key qualities ● Some people are not eligible, e.g. those with a criminal conviction, bankrupts, members of the forces and police	● Be on electoral register of area covered by court ● Have resided in UK for five years since 13th birthday ● Those with certain criminal convictions are disqualified ● Those in the administration of justice are ineligible
● Nominated or apply ● Interviewed by local advisory committee ● Appointed by Lord Chancellor	● Selected at random
● Given training and appraised	● Some are shown video of court – no other training
● Sit in Magistrates' Court ● Bench of two or three ● Hear summary and triable either way cases ● Also do some civil cases ● Specially trained magistrates sit in Youth Court	● Sit in Crown Court ● Panel of 12 ● Hear indictable and triable either way cases ● Can be used in some civil cases e.g. defamation in the High Court or County Court
● Decide verdict ● If defendant is guilty also decide sentence	● Decide verdict ● Judge decides sentence ● In civil cases decide amount of damages

13.1 LAY MAGISTRATES

13.1.1 Qualifications

1. On appointment a person must be between 21 and 65 years of age. It is, however, unlikely that a person under the age of 27 will be appointed.

2. They must live within 15 miles of the Commission area to which they are appointed.

3. Those with a criminal conviction, undischarged bankrupts, members of the forces, police officers and traffic wardens are not eligible.

4. In 1998 the Lord Chancellor set out six key qualities which candidates should have. These are:
   - good character;
   - understanding and communication;
   - social awareness;
   - maturity and sound temperament;
   - sound judgment;
   - commitment and reliability.

   Those appointed must be prepared to sit at least 26 times (and preferably 35 times) per year.

13.1.2 Appointment

1. Lay magistrates are appointed by the Lord Chancellor (or in Lancashire by the Chancellor of the Duchy of Lancaster) on behalf of the Queen.

2. The Lord Chancellor relies on recommendations made to him by local advisory committees.

3. Local groups (political parties, trade unions, chambers of commerce, etc.) put suitable candidates forward to the local advisory committees. In addition, the advisory committees can advertise for individuals in the local community to put themselves forward.

4. The local committees interview candidates and recommend suitable people to the Lord Chancellor.

5. In putting forward names the committee must also consider the composition of the local bench in terms of gender, ethnic origin, occupation and political views. The aim is to keep as good a balance as possible of different types of people.

6. Employers are obliged to give employees time off to sit as lay magistrates (s50 Employment Act 1996).

13.1.3 Composition of the bench

1. Despite the efforts at getting a good mix of people as lay magistrates, there is still a feeling that magistrates are 'middle-class, middle-aged and middle-minded' as the middle classes are over-represented.
2. Women are well represented, making up nearly half of all lay magistrates.
3. Ethnic minorities are still slightly under represented, though over the past few years more have been appointed.
4. There has been an effort to recruit disabled people to the bench and the first blind magistrates were appointed in 1998.

13.1.4 Training

1. Under the Lay Magistrates New Training Initiative (started 1998), newly appointed magistrates have to achieve four basic competencies. These are:
   * an applied understanding of the framework within which magistrates operate;
   * an ability to follow basic law and procedure;
   * an ability to think and act judicially;
   * an ability to work as an effective member of a team.
2. Each new magistrate keeps a Personal Development Log of their progress and has a mentor (an experienced magistrate) to assist them.
3. During the first two years of the new magistrate sitting in court, between eight and eleven of the sessions will be mentored. In the same period the magistrate is also expected to attend about seven training sessions.
4. Appraisals are held to check if magistrates have acquired the competencies.
5. This scheme involves practical training 'on the job'. It answers the criticisms of the old system where there was no check on whether magistrate had actually benefited from training sessions they attended.

13.1.5 Retirement and Removal

1. Lay magistrates cannot sit on the bench to hear cases after the age of 70, but are placed on the supplemental list.

2. The Lord Chancellor can remove a magistrate for good cause. The usual reason for removal is a criminal conviction, but some of the reasons have been criticised, e.g. removal for transvestite behaviour.

3. About ten lay magistrates are removed from office each year.

13.1.6 Role

1. Two or three lay magistrates sit together to form a bench. They have wide powers over criminal cases. They have jurisdiction to:
- try all summary offences;
- sentence those who are guilty (the maximum sentence is six months' imprisonment and the maximum fine is £5000);
- deal with mode of trial hearings for all triable either way offences, and try those which it is decided should be dealt with in the Magistrates' Court;
- deal with the first hearing of all indictable offences and then transfer those cases to the Crown Court;
- hear applications for bail;
- issue arrest and search warrants.

2. Specially trained lay magistrates also sit in the Youth Court.

3. Lay magistrates also have jurisdiction to deal with the following civil matters:
- licensing;
- enforcing demands for council tax;
- family cases.

4. Each bench is assisted by a Magistrates' Clerk who guides the magistrates on questions of law, practice and procedure.

13.1.7 Advantages

1. There is involvement of lay people with local knowledge.
2. Having three magistrates on a panel is likely to give a balanced view.
3. Magistrates comes from a greater cross-section of society than professional judges.
4. As they are only paid expenses the system is cheaper than using professional judges. A trial in the Magistrates' Court costs £1500 compared to £13,500 in the Crown Court.
5. Improved training and appraisal should improve the quality of the bench.
6. The Auld Review (2001) supports the continuing use of lay magistrates. It is likely to suggest that lay magistrates could sit with a District judge to hear slightly more serious cases with a maximum term of imprisonment of two years.

13.1.8 Disadvantages

1. There is a much higher conviction rate in the Magistrates' Court than in the Crown Court. This leads to allegations of bias in favour of the police and prosecution.
2. There is not a balanced cross-section of society as the middle classes are over-represented on the bench.
3. There is inconsistency in sentencing and granting bail. In 1996 the National Association of Probation Officers said that sentencing was a 'geographical lottery'. This claim was supported by statistics which showed that a defendant convicted of theft was three times more likely to be imprisoned in Folkestone than in Brighton.
4. Lay magistrates lack legal knowledge and may rely too heavily on the clerk.

13.2 JURIES

13.2.1 Use of juries

1. Juries are used in criminal cases in the Crown Court where the defendant pleads not guilty.
2. There is limited use of juries in civil cases in the High Court and County Court. The only civil cases in which there is a right to jury trial are defamation, false imprisonment, malicious prosecution and fraud.
3. Juries are used in the Coroners' Court to enquire into deaths occurring in prison, police custody, industrial accidents or circumstances where health and safety of the public is concerned.

13.2.2 Jury qualifications

1. The basic qualifications are laid down by the Juries Act 1974. These are that to serve on a jury a person must be:
   - aged between 18 and 70;
   - registered as a parliamentary or local government elector;
   - have been resident in the UK for at least five years since their thirteenth birthday.
2. In addition, people are disqualified from jury service if they:
   - have been sentenced to life imprisonment or a custodial sentence of five years or more;
   - have served any other custodial sentence or received a suspended prison sentence within the last ten years;
   - have been subject to a Community Service Order (Community Punishment Order) within the last ten years;
   - have been placed on probation (Community Rehabilitation Order) within the last five years;
   - are currently on bail.
3. Some categories of people are ineligible to serve on a jury. These include:
   - those suffering from mental disorder or who are not capable of managing their affairs;

- the judiciary;
- others who have been concerned in the administration of justice within the last ten years;
- religious ministers and members of religious communities.

4. Some people have the right to be excused from jury service. These include:
   - those over the age of 65;
   - those who have been on jury service during the past two years;
   - Members of Parliament;
   - members of the medical professions;
   - members of the forces.

5. Once summonsed for jury service it is possible to apply for discretionary excusal. This will only be granted if there is good reason, such as being too ill to attend. Jury service can also be deferred where the date given is inconvenient, e.g. because of examinations or business commitments.

13.2.3 Selection of a jury panel

1. Names are selected at random from the electoral register for the area in which the court is situated. The selection is done by computer at the Central Summoning Bureau.

2. Those names chosen may be vetted for criminal convictions via the police computer data of criminal records.

3. In exceptional cases, a juror's background and political affiliation may be vetted. This should only occur in cases involving national security or terrorism. The Attorney-General must give permission for vetting (Practice Note (Jury: Stand by: Jury Checks) (1988)).

4. At court both prosecution and defence can challenge individual jurors for cause (s12 Juries Act 1974).

5. There may also be a challenge to the array, i.e. the whole jury panel on the basis that it was chosen in an unrepresentative and biased way (s5 Juries Act 1974).

6. However, the fact that a jury does not contain any ethnic minority jurors is not a ground for challenge (*R v Ford* (1989)).

7. The prosecution may stand by individual jurors without giving a reason, but this right should be used sparingly (Practice Note (Jury: Stand by: Jury Checks) (1988)).

8. The judge may discharge any juror whom he thinks lacks the capacity at act effectively as a juror (s9 Juries Act 1974).

13.2.4 Problems with selection

1. Not all people, especially the young and ethnic minorities, are registered to vote. The use of the electoral register excludes these. It also excludes homeless people.

2. Although the selection is random, this may not produce a cross-section of society.

3. There are too many discretionary excusals – Home Office research (1999) found that one in every three jurors was excused. This further undermines the representativeness of the jury.

4. Vetting is considered an invasion of privacy, but the Court of Appeal has ruled that it is lawful (*R v Mason* (1980), *R v McCann* (1990)).

13.2.5 The role of the jury in criminal cases

1. A jury is used in less than 15% of criminal cases.

2. There is a split function between the judge and the jury. The jury decides the facts and the judge decides the law.

3. The jury decides the verdict of guilty or not guilty. If the defendant is found guilty the judge decides the sentence.

4. The judge cannot place pressure on the jury (*Bushell's case* (1670), *R v McKenna* (1960)).

5. The jury's verdict can be unanimous or, after at least two hours' deliberation, by a majority of 10 to 2 or 11 to 1.

6. Where the verdict is by majority, s17(3) Juries Act 1974 states that the foreman of the jury must state in court the number agreeing and the number disagreeing with the verdict. However, the Court of Appeal has held that provided the number agreeing with verdict is within the allowed majority,

there is no need for the foreman to also state how many disagreed (*R v Pigg* (1983)).

13.2.6 Advantages of juries

1. There is public involvement in the legal system which makes the system more open.
2. The defendant is tried by his peers.
3. There is public confidence in the use of juries.
4. They are 'the lamp that shows that freedom lives' (Lord Devlin).
5. The use of 12 jurors should cancel out any individual bias.
6. The jury is independent. This allows them to come to a 'just' verdict as opposed to a 'legal' verdict (*Ponting's case* (1985), *R v Randle and Pottle* (1991)).

13.2.7 Disadvantages of juries

1. The jury's decision is reached in secret. The reasons for that decision are not known.
2. In some cases the jury has used unreliable means of coming to a decision, e.g. in *R v Young* (1991), where a ouija board was used to contact the dead victims.
3. Jurors may be racially biased, as in *Sander v United Kingdom* (2000) where the European Court of Human Rights ruled that a jury should have been discharged.
4. Jurors may not be able to understand complicated cases. Both the Roskill Commission (1983) and the Auld Review (2001) have recommended that juries should not be used in complicated fraud cases.
5. Media coverage may influence a jury's verdict, especially in high profile cases.
6. The compulsory nature of jury service is unpopular.
7. Jurors can be nobbled.
8. Acquittal rates in the Crown Court are criticised for being too high. However, a large number of acquittals are directed by the judge. The jury acquits in about 36% of cases.
9. The use of a jury makes a case longer and more expensive.

13.2.8 Special problems of civil juries

1. In civil cases the jury decides the issue of liability and also the amount of damages to be paid.
2. Civil juries may be biased against newspapers or well-known personalities involved in libel cases.
3. The amount of damages is unpredictable and inconsistent. However, on appeal the Court of Appeal can substitute the amount they feel is proper (s8 Courts and Legal Services Act 1990).
4. Juries add very heavily to the costs of the case. The losing party is likely to face a bill of hundreds of thousands of pounds.

13.3 OTHER LAY PEOPLE IN THE SYSTEM

1. Lay members are used in tribunals. These will have knowledge of the type of cases heard by the particular tribunal.
2. Lay members with expert knowledge are also used in some of the specialist courts, such as the Restrictive Practices Court and the Admiralty Court.

CHAPTER 14

LEGAL SERVICES AND FUNDING

HELP FOR FUNDING

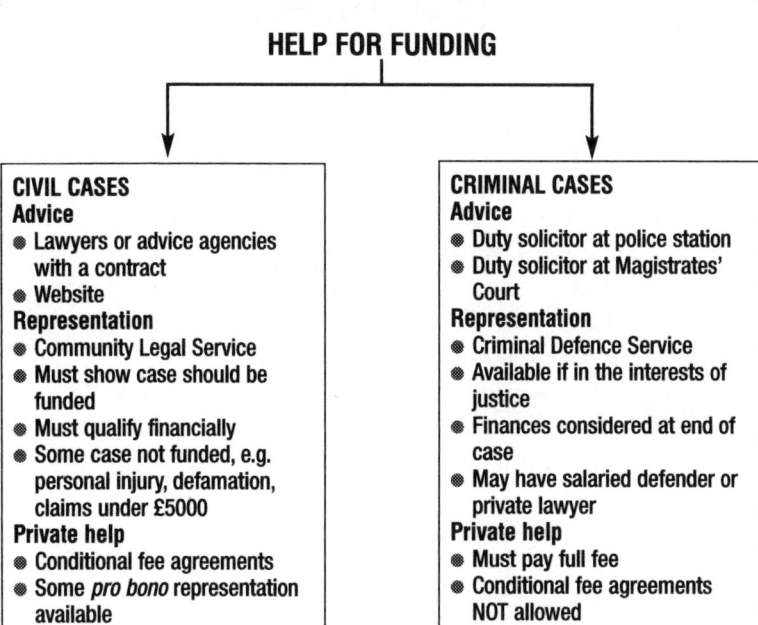

CIVIL CASES
Advice
- Lawyers or advice agencies with a contract
- Website

Representation
- Community Legal Service
- Must show case should be funded
- Must qualify financially
- Some case not funded, e.g. personal injury, defamation, claims under £5000

Private help
- Conditional fee agreements
- Some *pro bono* representation available

CRIMINAL CASES
Advice
- Duty solicitor at police station
- Duty solicitor at Magistrates' Court

Representation
- Criminal Defence Service
- Available if in the interests of justice
- Finances considered at end of case
- May have salaried defender or private lawyer

Private help
- Must pay full fee
- Conditional fee agreements NOT allowed

14.1 PUBLIC FUNDING FOR CIVIL CASES

Under the Access to Justice Act 1999, there are now two new schemes. These are the Community Legal Service for civil matters and the Criminal Defence Service for criminal cases. The Legal Services Commission oversees the public funding for both these schemes.

14.1.1 The Community Legal Service

1. The Community Legal Service provides the following services for matters involving civil law:

- general information about the law and legal system and the availability of legal services;
- legal advice;
- help in preventing or otherwise resolving disputes about legal rights and duties (this may include representation in the County Court or the High Court);
- help in enforcing decisions by which such disputes are resolved.

2. The money to pay for this service comes out of the Community Legal Fund. There is a set limit for the fund.

3. Certain types of civil cases are *not* funded by the Community Legal Services Fund. These include:
- claims for personal injury, or death or damage to property through someone else's negligence;
- defamation or malicious falsehood cases;
- claims for amounts of less than £5000;
- most tribunal hearings, except for cases in the Mental Health Tribunal and Immigration Tribunals.

14.1.2 Funding criteria

1. The person must show that their case should be funded. To decide this the following points are considered:
- the likely cost of funding and the benefit which may be obtained;
- the amount of money in the Community Legal Fund;
- the importance of the matters for the individual;
- the availability of other services (such as conditional fees);
- how likely it is that the case will be won; there must be a realistic chance of the case succeeding before public money is made available for it.

2. The person must qualify financially. To decide this their disposable income and disposable capital are calculated.

3. Disposable income is the amount of income available to a person after taking into account essential living expenses.

4. Disposable capital is the assets owned by the person. It includes the equitable value of the home above £100,000.

5. If disposable income and capital are below the minimum limits, the person will receive free funding. If their disposable income and capital are above the maximum allowed, then they do not qualify for help. If their disposable income and capital are between the minimum and maximum figures they will have to pay a contribution towards the cost of the funding.

14.1.3 Problems with funding of civil cases

1. Money is allocated to regional offices of the Commission according to the amount identified as necessary for that area. This could result in one area not having enough to fund all the cases it needs.

2. Very expensive cases are funded on a case-by-case basis through individually negotiated contracts from a central fund.

3. About 5000 firms of solicitors have contracts. This about half the number who previously did legal aid work. There are problems of access to justice in some areas where there is no solicitor doing publicly funded work.

4. Even solicitors who do publicly funded work are cutting back on the number of cases they take because of the low rates of pay.

5. The statutory charge (clawback) can mean that a claimant has very little left from their damages even though they won the case.

14.2 PRIVATE FUNDING FOR CIVIL CASES

Paying privately for a lawyer is very expensive, especially in London. Most individuals who do not qualify for help and representation under the Government scheme cannot afford to pay full private fees. For this reason conditional fee agreements have been developed.

14.2.1 Conditional fees

1. These were first allowed by the Courts and Legal Services Act 1990 and extended by the Access to Justice Act 1999.
2. The solicitor and client agree on the fee that would normally be charged for such a case, with a 'success fee' payable if the case is won.
3. If the solicitor does not win the case, then the client pays nothing. If the solicitor is successful then the client pays the normal fee plus the success fee.
4. The Access to Justice Act 1999 allows courts to order that the losing party pays the amount of the success fee to the winning party.
5. It is possible to insure against losing a case and, if the case is won, s29 Access to Justice Act 1999 allows the court to order the losing party to pay the cost of insurance premiums.

14.3 ADVICE AGENCIES

Free advice can be obtained from a number of agencies. Some of them specialise in a particular area of law, others give general advice. Some examples are:

- the Citizens' Advice Bureau;
- law centres;
- the Community Service Website.

14.4 THE CRIMINAL DEFENCE SERVICE

1. Since April 2001 the Criminal Defence Service has been responsible for the funding of criminal cases for defendants.
2. This service is aimed at 'securing that individuals involved in criminal investigations or proceedings have access to such advice, assistance and representation as the interests of justice require'.

14.4.1 Advice and assistance

1. There is a duty solicitor scheme for people who are arrested and held in custody at a police station. This is free.
2. When someone is arrested, the custody officer at the police station must tell them about this scheme.
3. There is also a duty solicitor scheme at many Magistrates' Courts for people to receive free advice on their cases. The solicitor may also represent them on matters such as bail applications.

14.4.2 Representation

1. The Legal Services Commission has the power to decide when a defendant should have a legal representative paid for by the State.
2. This is done by deciding if it is in the interests of justice for the defendant to be represented in court. Five categories are considered. These are whether:
   - the individual would, if any matter arising in the proceedings is decided against him, be likely to lose his liberty or livelihood or suffer serious damage to his reputation;
   - the determination of any matter arising in the proceedings may involve consideration of a substantial point of law;
   - the individual may be unable to understand the proceedings or to state his own case;
   - the proceedings may involve the tracing, interviewing or expert cross-examination of witnesses on behalf of the individual;
   - it is in the interests of another person that the individual is represented.
3. There are some salaried defenders working for the Criminal Defence Service. However, the defendant has a right to choose an independent lawyer, but only from those firms that have a contract with the Legal Services Commission.

4. At the end of a criminal case the defendant's financial position is considered to see how much, if anything, he should pay towards the cost of providing him with a lawyer.

14.4.3 Budget

There is no fixed budget and the funding of criminal cases is demand led. If the cost of criminal cases becomes very heavy, then it is possible for funds from the civil budget to be transferred to the criminal budget.

INDEX